AMERICA'S CHANGING WORKFORCE

ABOUT YOU, YOUR JOB AND YOUR CHANGING WORK ENVIRONMENT

NUVENTURES
CONSULTANTS, INC.

AMERICA'S CHANGING WORKFORCE
About You, Your Job, and Your Changing Work Environment

Library of Congress Catalog Card Number 90-61642
ISBN 0-9625632-1-8 $12.95

NUVENTURES® and its logo are registered trademarks
of NUVENTURES® Consultants, Inc.

NUVENTURES® Publishing is a division of NUVENTURES®
Consultants, Inc.
SAN 200-3805

HD
5724
.A499
1990

CONVENTION PRESENTATION

A fifty minute, 35mm Transparency Presentation of *"America's Changing Workforce - About You, Your Job, and Your Changing Work Environment"* is available for your next convention or company meeting.

For details, write or FAX:

Presentation Coordinator
NUVENTURES Consultants, Inc.
P.O. Box 2489
LaJolla, CA 92038-2489
FAX: 619-459-0569

Please include the name of your organization or company, location, and two alternative dates and times in your request.

CONTENTS

CONTENTS   PAGE

CONTENTS   PAGE

_____CHAPTER V
THE GROWING IMPORTANCE
OF MINORITIES   87

_____CHAPTER VI
TOMORROW'S TECHNOLOGICAL
DEVELOPMENTS   97

Our consulting firm has written hundreds of industry reports since our start-up in 1975. The great majority of these have been prepared on a very confidential basis for large multinational firms. We will be continuing to conduct industrial market research assignments for these clients. However, I felt it was time NUVENTURES wrote a business book which could be read by a great many people.

In selecting a topic, I wanted to produce a book that would be genuinely useful to the American business community and to our country at large.

In order to identify a topic which could meet this criteria, I invited every member of our staff to suggest ideas which might fulfill this goal. Over fifty topics were submitted. Additionally, we gathered suggestions from a selected group of business people nationwide.

After narrowing down the list of potential topics to the best eight, I commissioned our staff to perform a survey of business professionals to help us make the final selection. From this, there evolved one clear cut winner.

And with some concept modifications, "America's Changing Workforce" was born.

As a first step in preparing America's Changing Workforce, I organized a team of four long time staff members to perform the research and write this book for our company. These were: John Patton, Sheila Gosselin, Kim Bacchioni, and myself.

Each of us divided up a list of the nation's top Human Resource managers, and other leading executives. Over a period of several weeks, we proceeded to contact them for interviews. To all respondents we promised and gave anonymity in return for their insights and remarks of a more candid nature. Throughout this book, the reader will note that there are paraphrased quotations based upon these contacts.

After many weeks of research, the long process of writing and revision commenced. Some of us worked on generating supportive library and numerical research, while others concentrated on the writing. Eventually, each of us wrote at least one original draft of a chapter in this book.

After several revisions by the group of four writers, Ellen McNamara was assigned to start final editing, just as she has done for every final report in the fifteen year history of our company. She was also given the job of designing an appealing book format, one which, after a great deal of input from the four writers, we accepted.

We hope you like our work, and that many of the social and business issues which it raises will receive the attention of our nation before they are upon us. We also hope that this effort will help our readers prepare for the very competitive and challenging future which lies ahead. Thank you for purchasing our book.

Tom McNamara
President
NUVENTURES® Consultants, Inc.

OUR EVOLVING WORKFORCE

♦ **In the year 2000, over 141 million Americans will be going to work.** This is nearly two and a third times the number which were employed a half century ago. **However, the growth rate of new additions to the workforce will be slower in the 1990s than for any decade in the past fifty years.**

♦ **Most American companies are unprepared for the metamorphosis that will sweep their workforce during the 1990s.** As a result, they will find themselves with serious deficits in workforce talent unless they initiate a program to prepare for the future.

♦ **Most members of the American workforce casually expect that the 1990s will simply be another decade.** They are unaware that a new series of fundamental values are building which will affect their traditional benefits, opportunities for advancement, retirement age, and working environment.

Growth of the Workforce

In 1950, America put 62.2 million people to work. By 1990, we had doubled that workforce to an estimated 124.6 million people. By the turn of the century, there will be an estimated 141 million people working in the United States.

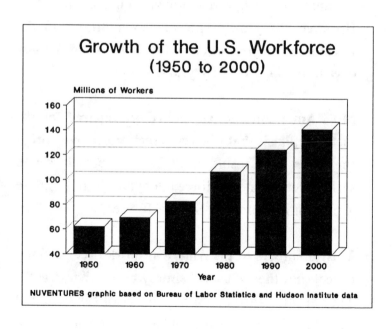

NUVENTURES graphic based on Bureau of Labor Statistics and Hudson Institute data

During the 1990s, there will be an additional 17 million people added to our workforce. Although this is a significant number of new people, **it will represent the slowest growth rate of the workforce in recent decades.** This is largely the result of a 1970s decline in the birth rate which will reappear in the 1990s in the form of a reduced number of people available for work. This shortfall in the number of new entrants into the workforce, coupled with a number of other changes, will have a dramatic impact on the 1990s.

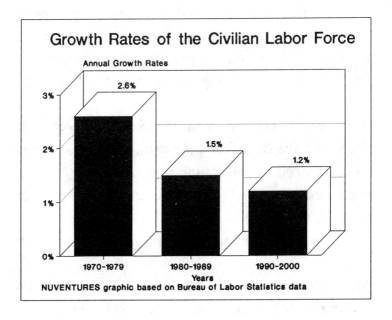

What the 1990s will Bring

The 1990s will bring us an enormous Skill Gap, one that will see companies drastically changing their recruitment patterns in order to find the talent they will need to compete in an increasingly competitive world market.

The 1990s will bring us a maturing workforce, one that will influence companies to alter their work patterns, and their health, pension, and other benefits programs. They will ask a certain percentage of their older employees to stay on the job past normal retirement age to replace the coming numerical and skill shortfall.

Women will represent a much greater proportion of the workforce than ever before. Individual companies will be forced to correct the salary disparity between the sexes, or they will be unable to attract the talent they will need to fill the jobs of the 1990s. Women will greatly influence the management styles of the 1990s.

Minorities will increase in importance within the workforce. In the future, companies will have to provide

4

more special training and education programs in order to help this diverse group attain fulfillment.

High technology will cause most companies' products to have a shorter marketable life. As new inventions replace the old at a quickening pace, companies will rise and fall with greater rapidity than ever before. Workers may be forced to change jobs several times during the 1990s without ever seeking to make a change.

America's share of the World's Gross National Product will continue to decline. America will no longer have as great a number of the world's largest companies headquartered within its borders. More Americans will be receiving paychecks from foreign owned companies than ever before.

High technology will help each worker to accomplish a greater number of tasks. Large groups of middle management will become obsolete. The opportunities for vertical promotion will decline. Companies will have to develop new strategies to reward good workers who they are unable to promote. The occupations which will be increasing at the greatest rate during the 1990s will be those which will require a higher educational background.

The workforce will be increasingly viewed as being composed of several distinct types of individuals each with special needs. Companies will allow their employees to select from among a "cafeteria" menu of available benefits to fulfill those needs.

Most of Us are Unprepared

From individuals to entire companies, the majority of Americans are largely unprepared for the great metamorphosis which will sweep their working environment during the 1990s.

With the exception of the educational shortfall, **most American companies have given comparatively little thought to the changes which will shape the immediate future.** Among the small number of companies who have looked ahead, very few have actually taken steps to prepare for the future.

Most people casually believe that the job that they have now will not change appreciably in the decade ahead. We hope that this book will help you understand the changes which will be occurring around you and why they are happening. We also hope that by reading this book you will be better prepared to fill a more important role in America's Changing Workforce.

EDUCATIONAL CHALLENGES

♦ A recent report concluded that there were **23 million functionally illiterate adults in the United States.** This same report gave 13% of our 17 year olds a similar designation.[1]

♦ **After 1993, the number of Bachelors Degrees awarded annually in the United States will decline.** Yet during the rest of the decade, a majority of all new jobs will require education beyond high school.[2]

♦ **Eighty percent of applicants from a large metropolitan area failed entry level examinations in basic reading and reasoning skills** when applying for a job with their local phone company.[3]

♦ **In an international assessment of math proficiency, U.S. 13 year olds scored lowest of those in all countries tested:** Korea, several Canadian provinces, Spain, the United Kingdom, and Ireland.

♦ A professional athlete testified before Congress that, **even though he had received a college degree, he could not read.**

Seriousness of the Problem

Currently there is no existing measure of academic comparisons for all of the nation's grammar and high school students. **But that achievement levels have declined is a fact of universal agreement.** What is happening to the average student by the time he or she graduates from high school and is ready to work can be exemplified by this story shared by one of the nation's leading personnel managers:

A Japanese manufacturer was setting up a new car production facility in the United States. The manufacturer had installed the same statistical quality control program that had been utilized very successfully for many years in Japan. As part of this system in Japan, production workers entered numerical data into a computer terminal after they had completed their designated tasks in the production line. In this way, inventory was always kept in good supply, and if there was difficulty fitting a particular nut or bolt, manufacturing tolerances were checked immediately. The job of entering this rather simple numerical data and some verbal commentary had been performed without a problem for many years by Japanese workers who were high school graduates.

However, when the system was installed in the U.S., a different situation evolved. After local high school graduates were hired to work in the new plant, it was quickly determined that they could not fulfill the quality control role which their Japanese employers had expected of them. In a nutshell, a high percentage of the workers were totally unable to reliably input data into the computer. Eventually, additional workers with a higher level of education were hired to fulfill the routine quality control function. The increased number of workers resulted in higher-than-anticipated production costs. Maybe of more significance, the situation greatly reduced the workers' opportunity to contribute their own ideas about the production process. This diminished the chance for production innovations and improvements in the system.

An indicator of the decline in education is the average Scholastic Aptitude Test (SAT) scores which are summarized over almost four decades on the following page.[4] These SAT scores show a long term decline in both verbal and math abilities of the nation's high school students interested in applying for college.

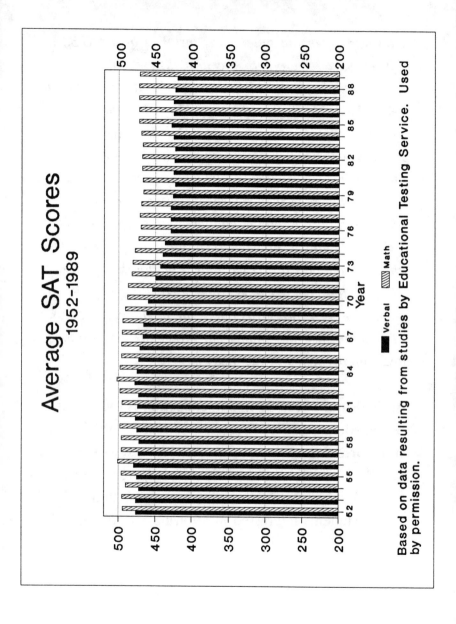

Average SAT Scores
1952-1989

Based on data resulting from studies by Educational Testing Service. Used by permission.

Educational Testing Service also assessed the math proficiency of 13 year olds in five countries and four Canadian provinces.[5] As shown in the graph below, **the math proficiency of U.S. students lagged behind that of students in all countries tested: Korea, Spain, the United Kingdom, and Ireland.** Students in several Canadian provinces also performed better than their U.S. counterparts on this test. Some of these countries cannot be considered as highly industrialized, but in terms of math proficiency, they seemingly would be able to offer potential employers a more trainable workforce.

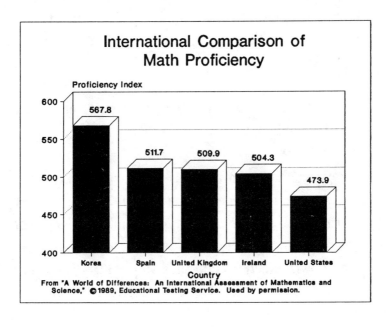

International Comparison of Math Proficiency

From "A World of Differences: An International Assessment of Mathematics and Science," © 1989, Educational Testing Service. Used by permission.

Another manifestation of the lack of mathematical capability among our minimum wage workforce is the use of symbols on cash registers in fast food chains. These symbol buttons represent specific types of hamburgers, shakes, fries, and other foods purchased by customers. No arithmetic is required of the worker. There are, of course, other reasons for the utilization of these simplistic devices, including inventory control and assuring honesty. However, the fact remains that part of the motivation behind installing these devices is that a significant number of employees cannot add and subtract with any degree of accuracy and consistency. The extensive use of Universal Bar codes in retail trades also minimizes the need for employees' mathematical skills and accuracy.

In the 1990s, technology will be utilized to eliminate many low end jobs.

♦ In early 1990, on a test basis, one leading fast food chain began installing automatic push button order terminals. This will eventually eliminate the need for many counter order takers, as customers simply push their own selections and then step up to the cashier to pay the bill and physically receive their orders.

The Root of the Problem - Declining Educational Values

That portion of the American workforce born between 1945 and 1955 had the benefit of a good education stressed to them by their parents more than any generation in the history of this country.

The parents of these 1945 to 1955 children had to endure the deprived economic climate of the Great Depression, followed by a terrible World War. When all of this strife was overcome, this hearty generation of young parents made it one of their credos that their children would not be denied the opportunities which fate had denied them.

For many a post-World War II American family, the goal of sending a first family member to college became paramount. And so by the early 1960s, America was sending its young people to college in numbers never before imagined. Competition to secure a freshman seat at a good university was keen in those years. Academic standards were high.

However, in the intervening years, many successive influences have lowered the quality and the quantity of the educational achievement of the American Nation.

Factors contributing to declining educational values have included, not necessarily in order of importance:

♦ Young Americans have increasingly become a *"video generation."* Television, video games, and other diversions have eclipsed reading for learning and entertainment. The resulting decrease in regularly shared family learning experiences has left students less prepared for academic pursuits, especially reading. This has had a particularly devastating effect on the middle class, which may not have sent their children to college, but which had traditionally been good readers.

♦ Increased **parental permissiveness** has allowed children to "do their own thing." This has not necessarily fostered rigid adherence to academic pursuits.

♦ **Increased use of drugs and alcohol** has become a manifestation of social decay.

♦ **A new wave of immigrants** has presented challenges to the educational system which it has been unable to deal with. Some immigrants did not master English after their arrival, and, as a result, often their children were ill prepared for academic achievement in the nation's schools. These children subsequently found less career success because they could not speak the English language. The cycle was and is self-perpetuating.

♦ **Standards have been reduced at many levels of education.** "Social" promotions sometimes replaced promotions based on academic achievement. By failing a student, the teacher was faced with the possibility of having to teach the same underachiever the following year. However, by passing the student on to the next grade, the underachiever became someone else's problem.

♦ **Legislators** who controlled the budgets for state institutions of higher education have often **pressured these schools to admit all "qualified" students.** This reduced competition for admission to these schools and failed to reward superior academic achievement by high school students.

♦ After the bulk of post-World War II babies passed through the higher education system, there were not as many members of succeeding generations to fill those seats. **Instead of reducing the number of freshmen seats available, some educational bureaucracies lowered standards in order to keep their classrooms full.** Furthermore, funding for many state colleges has been based on enrollment, and fewer students meant less funding for that institution. Many state governments exacerbated the problem by starting up even more colleges and universities. Ultimately, a college degree did not have the prestige it once commanded.

♦ **In addition to keeping classrooms full, colleges had a tendency to add new programs and advanced degrees, even when there was a shortage of qualified faculty.** This was done partly to attract increasingly scarce students by tailoring degree programs to the desires of these students. In part, this was also due to higher funding given by states to those institutions with a higher proportion of graduate students. New degree programs and graduate programs also boosted the academic reputation of the institution.

♦ **Teacher "burnout" and turnover,** due in part to poor pay for teachers, has led to many experienced professionals leaving the educational field. In Japan, the starting pay for school teachers exceeds that for any other public servant, and it is higher than or equal to that of engineers.[6]

All of these factors in different degrees have contributed to a decay in the educational values of the country as a whole.

Fewer College Graduates Just When More Education will be Required

Not only has the nation failed to produce as high a calibre of students as in the past, **but for the 1990s we will be producing fewer college graduates.** Shown in the following chart are historic trends and future projections of the number of Bachelors Degrees to be awarded through the year 2000.

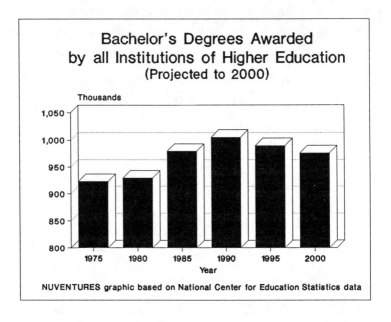

Bachelor's Degrees Awarded
by all Institutions of Higher Education
(Projected to 2000)

NUVENTURES graphic based on National Center for Education Statistics data

The number of Bachelor's Degrees awarded by all U.S. educational institutions is predicted to peak in 1993 and then decrease through 1998 before rebounding slightly in 1999 and 2000. The number of Master's Degrees is forecast to peak in 1992 and then decline throughout the rest of the decade.[7]

The major driving force behind this projection is the smaller size of the traditional college-age population

(18 to 24 year olds). This will be discussed in more detail in the following chapter.

While the educational clout of our nation is declining, our need for educated workers is increasing. A study commissioned by the Department of Labor (see graph below) indicates that more than half of the new jobs created in the nineties will require some education beyond high school.[8]

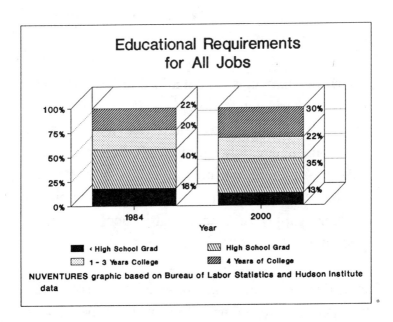

NUVENTURES graphic based on Bureau of Labor Statistics and Hudson Institute data

Corporate Strategies to Improve Education

President Bush began the 1990s with a State of the Union address calling for an improvement in the quality of the nation's educational system and by emphasizing the need for parental involvement in education. However, even if new government programs are instituted now with great devotion, it will be well into the 21st Century before we have a labor force fully impacted by such an effort.

American companies cannot afford to wait. However, the problem will not be so severe that one day personnel managers will look up from their desks and not be able to find any adequately educated people in the country at all. Yet there will be a critical shortage of fully capable, well educated applicants from among the available supply of recent high school and college graduates.

Individual companies will have different solutions to the educational dilemma. Most small and medium sized companies are presently doing little. However, some of the largest corporations are already addressing the problems. The activities undertaken vary greatly. Many are still in the experimental stage.

A few astute employers have recognized that the educational deficit problem is going to be put squarely in their laps during the 1990s, and that they will have to devise a way to cope with it or see their companies falter.

One universal theme, which personnel managers of leading companies expressed, was:

We recognize that we will either have to pay now to improve the education of America's workforce, or we will have to pay later when it will be more expensive.

These executives have identified at least four distinct types of programs evolving:

Business-Community Partnerships
In-House Basic Education
Early Recruitment of the Best Students
Worldwide Recruitment of Employees

Business-Community Partnerships

One strategy being used by some of the nation's largest corporations is to work within their own communities to influence the quality of education. The types of programs utilized have varied greatly. Some examples follow:

♦ In their headquarters city of St. Louis, General Dynamics has implemented a prototype program called "Access to Success." As part of this program, student teachers are funded by General Dynamics to encourage sixth, seventh, and eighth grade students in targeted sections of St. Louis to stay in school. The program directly seeks to counter peer pressure to leave school before graduation. Additionally, the project stresses the formation of math and science clubs among this age group. Ironically, despite General Dynamics' huge workforce across the nation, they do not employ a particularly large workforce in St. Louis. The company will likely reap few direct benefits from this program.

♦ A program titled "CHOICES," developed by the U S WEST Education Foundation (a nonprofit, non-endowed organization) in Seattle, Washington, is being presented in schools in 44 states by sponsors such as Hewlett-Packard, and many local phone and electric companies. Trained employee volunteers visit 8th and 9th grade classes and through creative exercises demonstrate the relevance of education in preparation for adult life and how education increases one's options.[9]

♦ More than 500 businesses, including Georgia Pacific, Motown Records, AT&T, Coca-Cola, K-mart, Nissan, Xerox, and Apple Computer have adopted 650 Los Angeles schools as part of that school district's **"Adopt-a-School"** program. These companies provide tutoring, career counseling, attendance and achievement incentives, club sponsorships, parent and teacher workshops, and student employment.

For example, McDonald's provided monthly attendance awards with tear-off coupons to motivate elementary school students to improve their attendance. Shell Oil presented special T-shirts and sun visors to junior high students with perfect attendance for one year.

Solar calculators and Disneyland passes were given to graduating ninth graders with three years of perfect attendance.

Kaiser Permanente Medical Center donated a life-size skeleton to a junior high and provided free blood pressure screening for the children, their parents, and faculty. Guest speakers are regularly provided to discuss such topics as food and nutrition, drug abuse, sports, medicine, and teenage pregnancy. Price Pfister donated 13 Apple computers to help fourth, fifth, and sixth graders master math concepts at their own individual rates.

♦ Harris Corporation sponsors seminars for teachers and students from kindergarten to high school. "Master" teachers expose local teachers to different instructional methods that may improve their educational performance. Student assemblies promote interest in science and math.

♦ Interlake in Chicago works with the existing educational system to improve their curriculum, and the quality of inner city education.

♦ American Cyanamid encourages its executives to tutor students in selected communities.

♦ Chrysler sponsors reading programs in Detroit public schools, and a volunteer program where employees go into the schools and instruct pupils.

♦ Many companies encourage their retirees to become involved in public school programs and are supplementing their pensions to do so.

Some of these programs are still in the experimental or formative stage, but they give a hint of things to come.

There are other illustrations of individual companies providing manpower and financial support for the educational institutions in their respective communities. But, perhaps even more significant is the example that successful business people can provide for students. As one executive put it:

Although businesses can provide experienced professionals to teach courses, more importantly, businesses can provide role models. These are successful people who can walk into a classroom and tell students that they, too, faced difficult circumstances when they were young, and tell students about how they overcame those difficulties to succeed.

Despite some good beginnings by selected organizations, many companies will not be able to financially contribute to the educational progress of their communities in a significant way. To financially support programs that will make permanent educational improvements takes a tremendous amount of money. Although companies with an exceptional year may be able to allocate some funds in this direction, overall they cannot be counted on to do so year in and year out.

Another reason why large public sector funding by private enterprise may not endure to a significant degree is that the economic dominance of large companies in America is forecast later in this book to decline. These larger companies will be eclipsed by smaller organizations unable to set up large scale programs.

Many medium and smaller companies have not yet become involved with our educational dilemma. One idea which would be useful to get them involved more deeply with local education efforts would be for there to be better tax incentives for the donation of used personal computers and possibly software to elementary and high schools. This credit needs to be more than just a recapture of depreciation. Businesses would then have the motivation to move on to the latest generation of computers a bit sooner, and the school systems would be the beneficiaries of very useful free training devices in the form of slightly older computers. It would also be an opportunity for smaller sized companies and the educational communities to introduce themselves to each other which might lead to other cooperations.

In-House Basic Education

Rather than supporting educational programs for a broad public sector, it is far more likely that the bulk of companies will look inward to build the intellectual capabilities of the people who work for them. This effort would contribute directly to the company's own progress, rather than being directed toward many people who may never work for the company at all.

That American businesses must provide remedial training for employees is a sad but actual fact:

♦ One large corporation has more than 30% of its hourly workforce enrolled in a company program teaching them elementary reading and writing.

♦ One-third of American corporations are today providing some form of basic educational training for their employees.[10]

Many companies, who are geographically dependent on a local labor force which is poorly educated, are planning intensive training programs to bring their own recruits up to an acceptable educational level:

One inner city company is planning to allocate as much as 80% to 90% of a new factory worker's first three to six months of employment time toward building up the basic educational background he or she should have received in public schools.

During this period, a new worker will be hired conditionally and receive educational training at a minimal wage. At the end of this period, if the recruit can pass a company-administered educational competence test, he or she will then be placed in a regular job.

This type of program will become very prevalent in the 1990s, especially among companies who recruit from geographic areas having low educational achievement.

At the same time, employers who are investing their resources to improve the education of employees will take steps to assure that workers receiving this training will continue with their company. They need assurance that employees will not go through a corporate educational improvement program and then leave to exploit their newly developed skills. **Employment Agreements, which bind the trainee to the company for some period of time after the training has been completed, will become more common in the 1990s.**

Early Recruitment of the Best Students

Another strategy of the 1990s will be to recruit the best potential talent well before their academic careers are completed. Some companies are targeting the top 20% of academic achievers in the high school graduating class. These students will be recruited, just like top football and basketball players are pursued by college sports teams. Those going to college will be offered scholarships, if they commit to working for that company upon graduation. For top high school students ready to join the workforce immediately, a number of "extra" benefits will be offered as an incentive to join a certain employer.

As one executive put it:

"We are in a very competitive world. We need the best raw talent in order to survive, and we are going to get it before someone else does. The other 80% [of potential workers] are going to be someone else's problem."

More and more employers will insist on applicants passing a company-administered test of basic skills as a condition of employment. It will no longer be adequate to apply for a job and depend upon a degree to demonstrate the skills an applicant possesses. A cottage industry that tutors people to pass qualification tests at leading employers may develop.

With the expected talent search concentrating on the top 20% of potential workers, *what is going to happen to the other 80% of tomorrow's workforce?* Unfortunately, the 1990s will be increasingly a world of the "haves" and "have nots", or more bluntly, a world of the "educated and able" versus the "left out." As one leading executive advised:

> *It is up to the parents to set the discipline and educational standards at home. No age is too early to start. Teachers are no longer allowed to discipline, out of fear of losing their job or worse. Tell your readers to get tough at home, and keep it up until the homework's done every night.*

Worldwide Recruitment of Employees

If the raw talent is just not there or is difficult to find in America, larger U.S. corporations will increasingly recruit from the huge pool of overseas talent during the 1990s. Because many corporations with only a few hundred employees now operate beyond U.S. borders, contact with overseas talent is more routine than ever before. Also, with an increasing number of foreign students expected to be attending U.S. colleges, it will be more common for U.S. companies to recruit them.

Our high standard of living makes America a very desirable destination for a skilled workforce to settle.

If a potential recruit has already spent time here as a student, he or she is easier to recruit.

As cited earlier, in many countries, average achievement levels in math and other capabilities far surpass those of United States students. **American companies will increasingly recruit from a worldwide pool of talent to obtain the best possible workers, even to a greater degree than in the past decade.**

Worldwide recruitment will not only be directed at potential managers. Companies in need of talented technicians, including aircraft maintenance personnel, machinists, carpenters, and others, will look outside our boundaries for the first time to obtain recruits for these positions.

Immigration laws will not successfully restrict recruitment of talented foreign workers by companies with at least a small overseas presence. These businesses can hire the employee first at an overseas facility. Then, the worker can be taken to the U.S. for training or transferred to work at a U.S. location with legal work permits to cover long "temporary" assignments. Eventually the employee can apply for citizenship. This practice has been going on for years and will be accelerating in the future.

The first impulse might be to advocate legislating against this practice, however to do so would not be in America's best interests. This would directly interfere with the viability of U.S. companies in an increasingly competitive world market. Multinational companies need foreign-born employees, who are familiar with the language and customs, to compete in overseas markets and to implement, from within U.S. headquarters, business plans and products that will find acceptance in foreign markets. The practice is also not unique to United States businesses. Worldwide, every company with multinational operations is finding an increasing number of its employees being of foreign birth.

New Directions in Education and Training

The 1990s will see companies placing a great deal of emphasis on many diverse forms of education and training for their employees.

Leading corporations are beginning to conduct employee seminars hosted by prominent psychologists and other experts on topics ranging from:

-*Managing stress between the job and the home*
-*The effects of drugs and alcohol on health*
-*The importance of bringing a good attitude*
  to the workplace
-*Corporate etiquette*
-*Teamwork in the workplace*
-*Healthy living*
-*Listening*
-*Corporate support of educational excellence*
  among our children

During late 1989, one of the nation's largest corporations was providing seminars for 2,000 workers per month in small groups. Employees were allowed to ask questions and interject their ideas, rather than just sitting and listening. The moderator simply kept the focus on the topic of the session.

As will be discussed in a later chapter, company medical clinics are also expected to be increasingly involved in providing Wellness Training Programs.

In the 1990s, there will be a continuing and even greater emphasis on employees taking courses toward additional degrees or for self-improvement. Companies will cooperate with colleges to give popular courses at the corporate location.

♦ For example, Kodak has certain courses telecast live via satellite into their Rochester facilities to save their employees from having to drive to a local college.

More companies will be sponsoring this type of education during the 1990s.

In addition to seminars, companies will use everything from posters to management reviews to influence positive attitudes in the workplace or office. Increasingly, companies understand that when an employee comes to work with a hostile attitude or creates a hostile environment in the workplace, the productivity of everyone around them suffers. **Companies operating in the 1990s will be placing the utmost emphasis on everyone getting along at work.**

Greater significance also will be put on training supervisors to recognize when pressure put on workers for productivity erodes to the point of becoming counterproductive.

Considerable emphasis will be placed on keeping up with change. The idea that one can be satisfied with the status quo will be drummed out of the corporate mentality. To a large extent, if we are still using the same software, computer system, office copier, or producing the same products we did three years ago, we are outmoded.

Keeping up with the newest developments in every profession is mandatory. Can you imagine going to a doctor who has not kept up with the latest medical advances? Consider that secretaries who could not adapt from the typewriter to the word processor are virtually gone. Look around your own office. Is there anyone left using a typewriter full time?

Corporate education programs of the future will also be directed at influencing such things as family values. More companies feel they need to motivate families to stress their children's educations. However, as one personnel executive put it: *"This is a tricky area, as corporations do not want to be accused of telling employees* *how to spend their off-duty hours. It has to be more subtle than that."*

At the same time, employers recognize that there will always be workers with the mentality of *"make your bucks and go home."* These employees will only do the minimum work possible and are resistant to any form of reeducation. **More sophisticated initial employee screening will focus more than ever before on identifying and avoiding hiring this type of employee.**

Suggestions for Educators

A number of business executives expressed frustration with the subject matter being taught in many of the nation's schools. The main comments centered around one theme:

Get back to basics, and teach them thoroughly.

Employers would like to see more high school graduates who can truly effectively read, write, and perform math. Almost every executive also stressed the need to encourage interest in the physical sciences. **Other subjects**

are necessary in creating a well rounded human being, but mastery of the basic skills should be the primary objective. If young employees possess these basic skills, then employers are in agreement that they can train them to sell, manage inventory, or assemble products. As one executive put it:

In the steel industry today, companies are doing remedial training of their employees. This puts a tremendous strain on companies that are operating in a highly competitive environment with intense foreign competition which has skilled labor.

If new employees have verbal skills and math skills, then they can be taught technical skills. The problem is not so much that people do not have technical training (from technical institutes, colleges, etc.) as much as they do not have the math and verbal skills to be trained in technical aspects of our industry. The schools must do a better job of teaching math and verbal skills. However, math skills are a must! Right now they are the great deficit.

Another manager commented:

Today's students are unprepared to enter the workforce because of poor learning skills. For too long, the choice for students has been to either go to college or to go to work. Educators must recognize that some students would benefit more from attending trade or technical schools than college. There needs to be more emphasis on educational levels between high school and college.

Furthermore, some employers stressed that **students need to be trained in the art of listening.** They felt this is an area completely overlooked in our educational process.

Some managers just shake their heads when it comes to the value of some college degrees. One director of a major corporation's Human Resources Department revealed his frustration by saying:

How many communications majors do we need? The universities know very well that only one in a thousand will ever get that job as a TV anchorman or a newspaper reporter. But they insist on training thousands and thousands for that one job.

41

How about offering more courses about business and how it works? How about seeing to it that our college students know simple math? They should not be permitted to graduate without a knowledge of the basics.

Ninety percent of those communications, history, and government majors will be sending in their resumes to me and my colleagues. They are ill prepared to do a job. They have only succeeded in finding a curriculum where they could avoid math, and there should not have been one available.

What we need is more resumes with a math, science, accounting, or even general business degree. Those are the people who get the good jobs. The others are fillers.

Chapter IX provides a good listing of the new jobs that will be added during the 1990s. It is based on readily available government statistics. Educators should be targeting a large percentage of their educational programs to train people to fill these new jobs. If this were to happen, our preparedness as an industrial nation would take a giant step forward.

CHAPTER III

AN AGING WORKFORCE

♦ In the 1990s, the U.S. population will be growing more slowly than at any time since the Great Depression.[1]

♦ The median age of the labor force will have risen from 34 years old in 1980, to 39 years old by the year 2000.[2]

♦ Between 1988 and 2000, the number of workers 25 to 34 years old will *decrease* by 11%, while the number of workers 45 to 54 years old will *increase* by 61%.[3]

The Ripple Effect _____

Our population growth has experienced several great ebbs and flows during the century. One extreme peak or valley will usually create succeeding ripples which resurface again and again for several generations until they finally become smoothed out by time. During the 1930s' Great Depression and World War II, there were relatively few children born. Consequently, twenty years later, in the 1950s and early 1960s there were fewer young people available to attend college and begin jobs.

Then came the opposite phenomenon. In the late 1940s and early 1950s, returning servicemen and prosperous merchants brought forth an unusual surge in the number of children born annually. Twenty years later, in the 1960s, we had an explosion in the number of people attending college and looking for first time jobs.

In the 1990s, we are going to see the reoccurrence of another valley caused in part by the original low birth rate of the 1930s and early 1940s. **This second generation cycle will confront us during the 1990s in the form of a much reduced number of entry level**

workers and college graduates. It is one of several key trends shaping the decade ahead.

Simultaneously, we are in the midst of an increase in the birth rate. Many of the 1970s college graduates and others decided to delay having children until their thirties. They are having them in the late 1980s and early 1990s, and hence the current great attention to child care as an important benefit.

Maturing of the Workforce

Since growth in the number of young adults will be tapering off in the 1990s, fewer youths will be entering the workforce or enrolling in college. As illustrated in the following graph, the number of high school graduates will decrease until 1992, and then the number will again start to climb. Notice that during the remainder of the century, the annual number of high school graduates will never again reach the levels of the late 1970s and early 1980s.

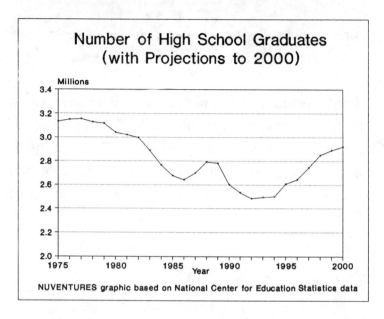

Number of High School Graduates
(with Projections to 2000)

NUVENTURES graphic based on National Center for Education Statistics data

For the period from 1988 to 2000, the number of 20 to 24 year olds in the workforce will shrink by more than 850,000, while the number of 25 to 34 year olds will decline by more than 3.8 million.

However, **the segment of the workforce 35 years and older will be growing.** The greatest increase will be in workers 45 to 54 years old, followed by those 35 to 44 years old. Workers in the 55 to 64 age group will grow by more than 1% each year. The estimated annual 1990s growth rates for each age group, drawn from the Bureau of Labor Statistics, are shown on the following chart.

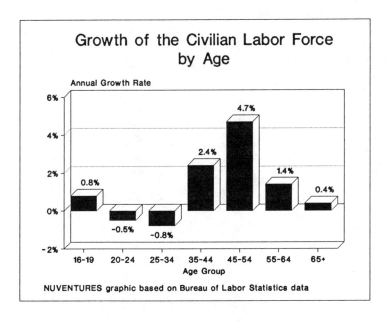

Growth of the Civilian Labor Force by Age

Annual Growth Rate

NUVENTURES graphic based on Bureau of Labor Statistics data

The bar chart on the following page shows the proportions that each age group in the workforce represented during two past years compared with a projection for the year 2000. **The most dramatic changes will be in the 45 to 54 year old group which represented only 16% of the 1988 workforce, but by the year 2000, the same age category will represent 22% of the civilian workforce.**

One of the most interesting features of this 45 to 54 year group is that a very high proportion of them will be women, who will be returning to the workforce.

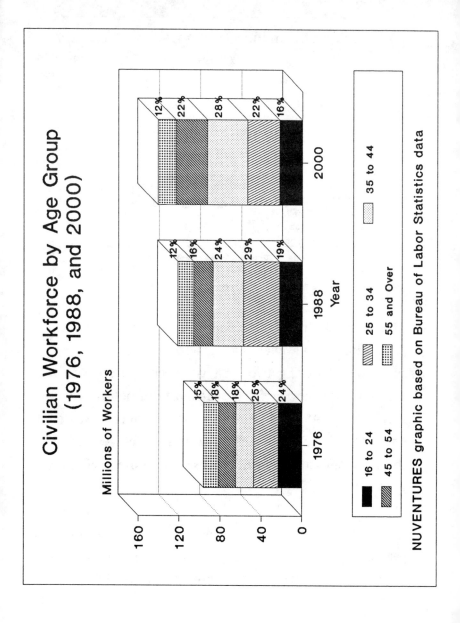

Civilian Workforce by Age Group
(1976, 1988, and 2000)

NUVENTURES graphic based on Bureau of Labor Statistics data

A Role for Our Mature Workers

With the projected shortfall in both the number and quality of high school and college graduates in the 1990s, mature workers represent one major source from which that shortfall can be made up. Some of our more talented mature workers will be asked to extend their careers during the 1990s and perhaps a bit into the new century. This will include inviting women who have raised a family to return to the workforce.

One leading Human Resources manager succinctly stated:

They will be a major source of the replacement talent we need. We have all been studying the problem. We will be preparing incentives to make it worthwhile for them to stay on the job a bit longer. By the late 1990s, we are really going to need these people.

The Psychological Preparation

We know we are getting older as a nation, and there is nothing we can do to prevent it. However, there is a great deal that we can do to prepare for it in the workplace.

The number one preparation which we will have to make is psychological. **Ironically, some of the generation which once was not going to trust anyone over 30, will now remain on the job well past normal retirement periods.**

Fortunately, we have had good preparation for the things which are to come. President Reagan served until he was 78. If President Bush completes a second term, he will be 72. Bob Hope and George Burns are still able to make us laugh with timely jokes. Nolan Ryan, an antiquated player by previous athletic standards, is still setting strike out records. The average life expectancy for both men and woman has moved firmly into the 70's, and with the almost daily advances in medicine and health care, life expectancies will be climbing higher and higher during the 1990s.

In the future, we are all going to be seeing a great many mature workers around the office and the factory. As many Human Resource managers indicated, we are going to need our skilled mature workers to fulfill certain deficits projected for the immediate future.

Desirable Traits of Mature Workers

One of the major reasons that we are going to need our older workers is that they have a level of education which, sadly, the new generation entering the workforce lacks. During the 1990s, we will be participating more firmly in a global economy, and we will be greatly in need of their education, as well as the experience factor which many of our older workers possess.

The vice president of a billion-dollar company expressed a commonly felt remark about mature workers:

We see older workers as having certain very desirable qualities. They are generally more educated and certainly less prone to making errors of judgement. They know how to get along in the business world. The over-55-year-olds are less likely to have a drug or serious alcohol problem. Also, older people don't have the same unreasonable expectations as young people entering the workforce for the first time.

Yet another personnel manager expressed these sentiments:

These older workers are usually very loyal, and after 25 years with the company, they know their way around. They need to be shown that they are still valuable and to be encouraged to adapt through continuous retraining. This is especially important at higher management levels.

Employers looking at the prospective workforce are going to be understandably bleak about the numbers of talented young people available. And they will face fierce competition to attract the most talented young workers to join their company.

Companies will often find that they can expand their workforce at a much reduced cost by encouraging older workers to stay on the job a few years longer.

For some who left the job market during the 1980s, an inability to cope with the high tech age was a major motivating factor. The rapidly changing technology left in its wake many frustrated workers who could not work with computers and the massive changes they brought about. However, by the year 2000, most remaining mature workers will have already proven that they can function in the rapidly changing technological environment, by virtue of their having already survived the computer and electronics revolution of the 1980s and 1990s.

Will Mature Workers
Want to Continue Working

One Human Resources executive commented:

The 1990s mature generation will have all the money, education, and power they need. Many of them have good pensions or other retirement benefits. Getting them back to work will be a challenge.

It is very likely that companies will not be as generous with their pension fund benefits in the 1990s as they had been in the 1970s and 1980s. As companies begin to realize that they will need to persuade some members of the workforce to remain on the job longer, they will recognize that they have created a group of retirees who are so well off that they cannot be enticed back to work. This will drive many employers to reduce pension fund benefits so as not to perpetuate this syndrome.

In addition, many mature employees have invested a substantial amount of overtime in building their careers, with a view toward retiring in their 50's (or even earlier). Part of their justification for putting so much "extra" time into their careers (time that could have been spent on family or leisure activities) is that they could build financial security at a relatively early age and be free to do whatever they liked. It is unlikely that businesses can do anything to entice employees with this mind set to remain on the job.

Current government policies and some internal company policies have been literally forcing qualified mature people to retire from the workforce, even when they might have wanted to stay on the job longer.

One of the major barriers keeping mature workers from staying on the job or coming back to work is our government's rather outmoded tax policies which are tending to make each potential retiree to consider:

Is it really worth it for me to continue working? How much of the new money I earn will I be able to keep?

♦ In an example shown in a special 1989 edition of Money Magazine, a 65 year old worker, who had $20,000 from retirement and other benefits as a base, decides to remain on a job to earn another $30,000 per year, but winds up losing the equivalent of three quarters of that additional salary to taxes and indirect taxes in the form of Federal and State taxes, and FICA, lost Social Security benefits, and a Medicare surcharge.[4]

Other barriers to continue working include the fact that most pension fund recipients cannot forestall maximum distributions to any later age than 70 1/2 years. Social Security payments must also be taken at age 68. So, for an employee who is considering coming back or continuing to work, he or she may currently find that adding money earned from the job to benefits income puts them into a higher tax bracket which yields a very slim net return.

A better system for our government to consider might be to let individuals store all benefits due them, even from Social Security, into special Keogh type accounts until they need it, and let it be taxed only when it is withdrawn. This would help shore up needed cash reserves in the nation's savings institutions. It would also allow those in the workforce to be able to work as long as they need, without unfair disincentives to work. As the nation's need for a contribution from the older workforce becomes more apparent, public pressure will hopefully cause some changes in the current system.

Identifying benefits which will appeal most to people of different age brackets has been left for the later chapter on Benefits. However, a few that are certain to be of importance in retaining the older generation include: **Primary Health Care, Elder Care, Life Insurance, Estate Planning, and Fulfillment of Social Needs.**

Motivations for Extending Careers

Companies and individuals are going to have to become more sensitive to the needs of older citizens. By understanding their needs employers will be able to motivate them to stay on the job longer or to return to work.

Some reasons why people might want to continue to work are:

♦ Some literally do not know what to do with themselves once the opportunity to work is no longer there. One concern of the mature worker is that they will no longer be useful or wanted.

♦ They may have only recently achieved those goals and challenges they have pursued throughout their entire career.

♦ By working, they can retain power, rather than becoming powerless.

♦ With people living longer, some workers will need the income to care for parents or other loved ones who are in poor health or unable to care for themselves.

♦ By working, they can retain their employer's health insurance coverage. This is especially important for particular health problems like diabetes, where it is difficult to find an insurance company who will cover a mature individual at a moderate cost.

♦ Some fear that Social Security and other retirement benefits will not come as promised or will be insufficient to cover their actual needs.

♦ Some, who have lost a spouse, need the companionship which the workplace gives them.

♦ Stories abound about peers who have left work and died very shortly thereafter.

By developing programs which help satisfy these aspirations and concerns, employers will find it easier to recruit or retain mature workers. As a Human Resources executive from the energy industry said:

Companies that do not have a systematic approach to accommodate the aging workforce are not going to hold on to qualified people because these people will be looking for companies who offer some type of reciprocity.

Managing a mature workforce will not be unusually difficult, but companies and individuals are going to have to be sensitive to their needs.

Rising Health Care Costs in Connection with an Aging Workforce

Having a greater proportion of mature workers will increase the use of the health care benefit. All American companies will see their health care costs escalate as the workforce ages. In the Benefits chapter, several trends in connection with reducing the spiraling cost of health care are noted.

There might be a need for government to consider providing private industry with credits for health care benefits paid workers above a certain age or financial level. If older workers are to become a greater proportion of the workforce, then employers will be taking the burden off Medicare and other public health programs in the interim. If this concession is not made, U.S. employers will become increasingly less competitive in the global economy.

Increasing Importance of Part Time Workers

Many older citizens will not want to, or be able to work full time. Once they realize the tax consequences of adding a full week's salary to accrued benefits and outside income, many may not find it attractive to work a full schedule. However, they may be willing to work part time. Employers will need to be willing to make compromises with employees about their hours. Inevitability, there will be many more part time workers from among the older generation.

Among service or production workers, scheduling hours on or off will be relatively easy. Some employers have already begun to utilize part time workers to a greater extent in order to avoid extending benefits which they would otherwise have to give to a full time worker. In the future, it will very likely become standard practice, and perhaps even law, to extend benefits to people in proportion to the number of hours that they actually work.

♦ One of the nation's leading service companies has a pilot program where they schedule "permanent part time" people to clean certain offices each week. In addition to an hourly salary, these workers are given a monetary benefit package in proportion to their monthly salary. For example, if an employee earns $1,000 per month they are entitled to 15% or $150 per month in benefits. The part time worker can then choose from among a list of benefits each with a set monetary value that in total cannot exceed their entitlement.

♦ Since the late 1980s, many of the leading fast food chains have been actively employing the older workforce. They are available to work the lunch hours, which a high school student cannot.

Service and production jobs can often be divided into a series of tasks that can be as effectively accomplished by two or more part time workers as by one full time employee.

Fitting white collar workers into jobs taking up only a proportion of a full work week will be much more difficult and will represent a greater management challenge for companies. The problem is that the mature part timer will not always be on hand. And in their absence, decisions are sometimes going to have to be made.

The best solution to this may be to find the mature part time white collar worker a discrete finite job that he or she can perform within the agreed upon hours of a reduced work week. This usually will mean that this class of worker might have to be taken out of the policy making positions that they might have previously held when they were full time employees. Some employees' egos will not be able to tolerate this, driving them towards the second career phenomenon which will be discussed shortly.

♦ One extremely important job assignment for the part time older worker would be to help with the growing educational training needs within companies. As was discussed in the Education chapter, there will be a great need for companies to conduct large scale remedial and other training programs for new employees. Because of their high experience levels, older employees could be the best choice for this type of assignment.

Another very useful idea is to have an experienced senior sit in on important management meetings. All too often a hot new management idea can turn out to have been tried 15 years ago, and having the experienced people on hand who have been through it once before, can save a lot of wasted motion.

In the decade ahead, there will be a tremendous shift toward the use of part time help. Much of it will be motivated by the Aging phenomenon.

♦ One index of this shift, is that in 1987 Kelly Services began recruiting retirees to fill its temporary positions. In that year, the 55 year olds or older represented 7% of their employees, by 1989 it had grown to 12%.[5]

Lateral Mobility Strategies

Some mature workers do not want to retire, but they no longer want to face the everyday stress associated with more demanding positions.

Companies are retaining these employees by offering lateral moves to less demanding positions. For example:

♦ An office equipment manufacturer allows unionized hourly workers who meet certain age and time-in-service requirements to bid on jobs with lower stress or fewer physical demands.[6]

In the coming decade, even more businesses will use similar strategies to retain mature employees. As one Human Resources executive said:

Some managers no longer want to handle the responsibility and risk that is associated with their managerial positions. Up to now, a rule of "up or out" has been utilized in many companies. Employees earn promotions or they are eliminated. However, this type of stress producing philosophy will very likely change. Employers must be willing to let mature employees step back into less stressful positions within the same company, perhaps in a mentor program. They will have less responsibility and less risk, and would receive less monetary compensation. Hopefully, these employees will stay with the same company, rather than seeking a less responsible position with a different firm.

Drawing From a Smaller Geographic Area

One of the consequences of an aging workforce is that more and more companies will need to recruit from the local population. In the past, the most prominent corporations have always had the luxury of recruiting from far and wide. They will still do this for their younger workers, but now with an increasing proportion of the population being older, they will find that they will need to rely more on the local population for their recruitment base.

Older people, for the most part will have more roots established in a community and will be more reluctant to leave. Thus, recruiting a mature person away from relatives, clubs, community positions, etc. will be difficult. Additionally, there may be a spouse to consider who has their own ties to the community, and their own responsibilities.

Another reason for a stiffening resistance against relocation is that many of our local communities have become much more attractive places to live during the past decade. Across the nation many communities which used to be culturally lacking are increasing in their repertoire of activities. Fewer people can be attracted away from where they live because of a sheer environment factor, excepting for a move to certain sun belt areas.

Second Career Executives

A phenomenon which will be emerging more strongly during the 1990s because of the greater proportion of mature workers, will be the emergence of the second career executive.

This is the determined, successful achiever who just does not want to retire. He or she may become frustrated with limited advancement opportunities at their long-time employer because top management has no imminent plans to step aside, or they simply may want to do something entirely different. This person typically has a sizable nest egg and will pursue a second career which is more "what I want to do" than the first.

♦ A leading chemical company executive, who for many years headed with great professionalism the market research function of a corporate division, moved to Chicago upon retiring. There, in cooperation with his daughter, he set up a market research firm exclusively for children's products. This executive used his original background, but he redirected himself to a target market with new opportunities and experiences. He was also, for the first time in his life, his own boss.

♦ A meat industry executive established his own consulting practice and newsletter dealing with labor issues affecting that industry.

♦ A former board member of a leading metals producer left his industry altogether and turned his gardening hobby into a chain of successful nurseries in the South.

With more executives having good pension fund benefits, paid mortgages, and children out of school, it is likely that many will "retire" in their 50's and work several years in another endeavor.

Many will be information generators or consultants in the industry where they previously worked. Others will focus on turning hobbies (woodworking, cooking, gardening, and travel) into jobs.

Many of them will work at home because it requires less capital during the difficult start-up stage. In addition, they can work at their own pace without feeling pressure to show up every day at an office.

Some very successful new companies will be started by second career executives during the 1990s.

WOMEN IN THE WORKFORCE

♦ **Nearly 63% of women 16 years old and older will be employed outside the home in the year 2000.** In 1976, only 47% of this group were working outside the home.[1]

♦ From 1988 to 2000, **the annual growth rate of the women's labor force will be almost double that of men.**[2]

♦ In 1972, women owned less than 5% of American businesses. By 1986, 30% of sole proprietorships were owned by women. **By the year 2000, more than 40% are expected to be owned by women.**[3]

♦ **Businesses adapting their working environment to accommodate the rights and needs of women will be a major trend of the 1990s.**

More Women will be Entering the Workforce

The number of women in the workforce is forecast to increase at an annual rate of 1.7%, almost twice the growth rate expected for men.

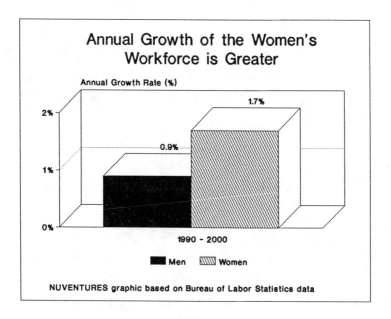

By the year 2000, 12 million more women will be working than in 1988. At the beginning of the 21st Century, women will represent 47% of our nation's labor force.

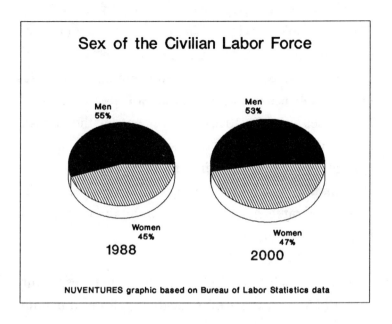

Sex of the Civilian Labor Force

Men 55%
Women 45%
1988

Men 53%
Women 47%
2000

NUVENTURES graphic based on Bureau of Labor Statistics data

Furthermore, **greater numbers of women are moving into ownership and management of businesses, and into skill areas where they have traditionally been under represented.** An executive of a leading steel producer said:

In the steel industry today, it is difficult to find a job that women cannot do. Most production jobs are driven by technology: computers and robotics. Women will move more and more into manufacturing industries.

71

Women are becoming an increasingly important part of our nation's workforce. With more women entering the labor force and, at the same time, the labor force growing more slowly, **competition among companies for accomplished women employees will greatly intensify.** Businesses are going to have to concentrate their efforts to attract and retain this diverse group, which includes college graduates, working mothers, second career women, and women reentering the workforce. Implementing strategies to attract and retain women will become more urgent.

Opportunities for professional advancement, especially for women who are well educated, will be abundant.

A New Business Culture

More than ever, women will be scrutinizing companies to select those who have implemented policies that are sensitive to their needs. **For some businesses, this will require a willingness to change to a new company culture that reflects the diversity of the evolving workforce and**

a reshaping of what some have characterized as a traditional white male system.

The new business culture will promote and sustain the variety of approaches which a diverse worker pool will employ in accomplishing their goals. As the Human Resources Vice President of one of the 50 largest corporations in America stated:

Different groups bring diverse backgrounds and experiences to the workplace. Our best salespeople are women. They are driven, successful, and have different methods of doing things. There are many alternative paths to the same outcome, just like the long distance switching system has many ways to route a telephone call to its destination. All businesses must have the flexibility to let their workers try different approaches.

Companies that successfully incorporate alternative problem solving approaches will have a competitive advantage. They will create a more comfortable work atmosphere that does away with the pressure to attack obstacles in a narrowly prescribed, predetermined manner.

Furthermore, early success in creating an adaptive, flexible environment will lead to even greater success over the long term. Women first up the management ladder will serve as role models and mentors for others behind them. Then, **the best potential women employees will gravitate toward companies where women have a tradition of being promoted to high level positions and where women executives can serve as role models to young aspiring workers.**

Women's Salaries

Traditionally, women have long been denied equal pay for equal work. Data from the Bureau of Labor Statistics confirms that by and large women are paid less.

In 1987, full time women employees received only 70.2% of the salaries of full time males. In Managerial and Professional jobs, the ratio was slightly lower at 69.8%.

The good news about this statistic is that the ratio rose dramatically in the 1980s. During all the 1960s and 1970s

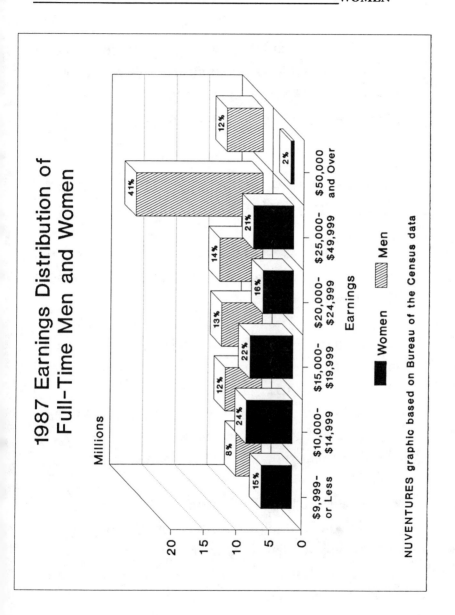

1987 Earnings Distribution of Full-Time Men and Women

Millions

NUVENTURES graphic based on Bureau of the Census data

Women   Men

Earnings

$9,999- or Less: 15%, 8%
$10,000-$14,999: 24%, 12%
$15,000-$19,999: 22%, 13%
$20,000-$24,999: 16%, 16%
$25,000-$49,999: 21%, 14%, 41%
$50,000 and Over: 2%, 12%

the ratio was about 60%. So, although there is a long way to go, the projected shortfall in qualified employees during the 1990s will help further close the salary differential between women and men.

Attracting and
Retaining Working Mothers

Working mothers will be looking for companies with policies that help them balance career and family obligations.

But practices that are sensitive to family needs are not important solely to women. With the increase in the number of two career families, the job of parenting has become a more equal partnership compared to past generations. Fathers are increasingly attracted to businesses that support family concerns.

♦ A recent study by DuPont found that 25% of men and about 50% of women had considered finding a new employer that offered more accommodating work or family flexibility. Nearly half of those who were using or planning to use child care were men.[4]

Flexible scheduling, part time employment, job sharing, parental leaves, working out of the home, and child care assistance are some of the major accommodations working families will be seeking in the 1990s.

Flexible Scheduling

Instead of the traditional "9 to 5" routine, flexible scheduling of office hours will allow workers to spend time when it is most needed with their children. Starting a job two or three hours earlier permits workers to pick up their children from school and have afternoons together. Late afternoon or early morning hours away from work let the employee take children to the doctor or make other appointments that need to be scheduled during traditional business hours. Starting work later gives family members an opportunity to take the children to school before going to work.

♦ Many IBM employees can start work one hour earlier or later than the normal schedule to allow for family care needs.[5]

In addition, more companies are permitting their employees to use sick leave and varying increments of vacation time to care for dependents. This gives additional flexibility to their scheduling.

Part Time Employment and Job Sharing

Many parents do not want to lose the challenge of the work environment but want to care for their children during their early stages of development. Part time jobs and job sharing will be partial solutions to this dilemma.

Letting employees with family responsibilities reduce their hours, rather than quitting entirely, keeps the benefits of their experience and training on the job. These workers stay up-to-date with the latest developments, alleviating retraining costs that otherwise might be required. These workers have greater energy and motivation toward the end of their shifts because they work fewer hours, and job "burnout" is less likely to occur. Also, absenteeism is generally not a problem because employees have the flexibility to take care of pressing concerns.

Job sharing, which splits a position among permanent part time workers, will gain greater acceptance. When different employees share the responsibilities of a job, the firm can capitalize on the strengths of both employees. Moreover, when one employee of a shared job quits, the position is still half filled, and the other worker can help select and train the replacement.

As with full time workers with families, scheduling flexibility will be a key consideration when a job is shared. Some workers will prefer half day shifts; others will want to split the week, with each member of the team working two-and-one-half days. Still others might elect to alternate their working weeks.

However, there are drawbacks to having more part time workers such as increased record keeping. Communication and coordination becomes more difficult, as there are more people working shorter shifts. Companies will have to make difficult decisions about the level of benefits these employees will receive. And firms will have to be careful not to relegate part time workers to menial tasks without paths for advancement.

Parental Leave

Parental leave programs will appeal to working mothers. These leaves allow parents to take time off for family care needs and assures that a similar position will be available when they return.

♦ IBM offers unpaid leaves of one to three years. Employees can take off the first year, but they must be available to work part time during the second and third years. While on leave, they still receive company-paid benefits.[6]

Child Care

As the number of women entering the workforce rose during the 1980s, so did concern over who would take care of the children. In this new decade, child care is in the forefront of concern for working parents. The choice of who to work for and even the decision to stay in the labor force will largely depend on the access working mothers have to quality, affordable child care.

Referral services, pre-tax employee deductions for child care expenses, child care subsidies, or employer-sponsored child care will be adopted by most companies to help meet the needs of the changing American workforce.

Referral services, which can be established with a modest investment, will be provided by both large and small businesses. These services will help parents find child care providers in their areas and guide them in evaluating that care. Information such as the location and size of the facilities, children's ages, vacancies, types of educational programs, and cost will be maintained to help working parents make better child care decisions.

Almost all larger companies will offer their employees the option of deducting child care expenses as part of a "cafeteria style" benefits plan. By deducting these expenses in a benefits plan, workers do not pay income tax on this expenditure. However, by electing to receive this benefit, parents must forego other benefits in the flexible plan. This will be discussed in greater detail in the Benefits chapter.

Some larger employers will directly subsidize their workers' child care expenses. Most often, employees earning less than a specified salary level will be reimbursed a portion of their cost for child care. In a few cases, companies will reimburse child care expenses for all employees. By subsidizing these costs rather than providing child care directly, companies do not incur liability for this service, and parents have flexibility in choosing their child care provider.

In limited situations, businesses will provide on-site child care for their workers. However, the investment required to establish a company operated child care facility is sizable, and most business executives feel that community based child care is more efficient. One manager stated:

> *In general, corporate child care on-premises will not happen. A company's own child care facility would not be efficient or profitable, because it would face no competition. With no competition, there is little incentive for efficiency. There are extensive child care systems already in place in most communities, and the principal growth in child care will come from community based providers.*

Others do not share this opinion. An opposing viewpoint was expressed by an executive in this way:

Company operated child care will play a bigger role. There will be many more corporate child care facilities, and the payback will be less lost time because mothers are traditionally the ones to take sick children to the doctor or to stay at home when the child care provider is unable to keep the children.

On-site child care facilities will be set up most rapidly where the company faces a critical shortage of workers and needs this benefit to attract the best employees.

Companies that provide for the needs of working mothers, and of working parents in general, by adopting flexible and part time scheduling, parental leave, working at home, and child care assistance will enable these workers to maintain and increase their valuable contribution to the American economy.

Attracting Women who are Reentering the Workforce

In the 1990s, the greatest growth in the women's workforce will be from the group between the ages of 45 and 54. Many of these will be well educated women who are returning to the workforce after taking time off to meet family obligations. This group will be an important pool of valuable employees.

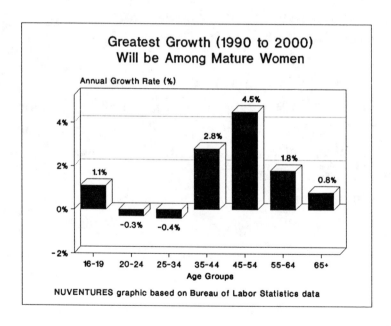

Greatest Growth (1990 to 2000) Will be Among Mature Women

Annual Growth Rate (%)

NUVENTURES graphic based on Bureau of Labor Statistics data

In addition to being well educated, many mature women have acquired considerable skills, like accounting and budgeting, negotiating, managing time, and setting priorities, while running their households. However, some will not be familiar with advances in technology made during their time away from the workplace. To facilitate the return of these workers, companies will have to establish programs to retrain and bring returning workers up-to-date with the latest developments.

Some businesses will also provide self esteem programs and workshops that orient returning women to the new work atmosphere, helping them get over any initial doubts and recognizing their skills and unique qualities.

Second Career Women

Some women, and men as well, will be looking to begin a new occupation. They may have set different personal goals, desired a change of pace, or relocated to accommodate a job change by a spouse. These second career workers will possess a great deal of experience and ability as a result of their former vocations, and they will be a valuable resource to prospective employers.

Many will want to fulfill long delayed aspirations in professions that are more personally satisfying and rewarding. A second career may represent a way to satisfy more esoteric pursuits outside the workplace, such as traveling, writing, or lecturing. Certainly, monetary reward will not be as important to some as individual gratification and accomplishment from their work.

In conclusion, companies that successfully incorporate women as a permanent part of the business culture will enjoy the benefits of a committed and determined group of workers.

THE GROWING IMPORTANCE
OF MINORITIES

♦ Sixty-one percent of workers entering the labor force during the 1990s will be minorities. The White male worker will represent only 30% of new employees.

♦ Hispanics will be the fastest growing group in the labor force. The Hispanic workforce will grow almost four times faster than the White workforce. The Black workforce will grow at almost double the rate of the White workforce.

♦ Minorities will face a critical decade. In order for them to attain their full potential within the American workforce, greater emphasis will have to be placed on improving educational levels.

More Minorities will be Entering the Workforce

Sixty-one percent of the over 17 million jobs which will be added during the 1990s will be filled by minorities. Specifically, 5.3 million are projected to be filled by Hispanics, 3.3 million by Blacks, and 2.0 million by Asians and other minorities.

The 1990s annual growth rate will be greatest for Hispanics at 4%. Blacks will have a 2% annual growth rate, while Whites will increase their numbers in the workforce by only 1% per year.

By the year 2000, the composition of our labor force is projected to be 74% White, 12% Black, 10% Hispanic, and 4% Asian and others including American Indians, Pacific Islanders, and Alaskan natives.

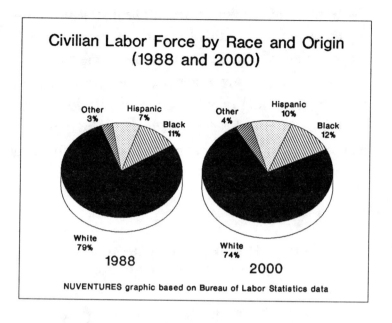

Civilian Labor Force by Race and Origin
(1988 and 2000)

NUVENTURES graphic based on Bureau of Labor Statistics data

The Educational Challenge
Facing Minorities

Fast changing technology and increased global competition will create more jobs that demand higher educational
and skill levels than ever before. As indicated in a
previous chapter, over half of the new jobs during the
1990s will require educational achievement past high
school.

Sadly, many of our minorities will be unable to qualify for those jobs unless there is a drastic turnaround in our educational system. For example, in the latest year for which statistics are available, 77% of White, while 65% of Black, and only 55% of Hispanic youths had graduated from high school. This disparity is not just a one year phenomenon, but has been going on for many years.

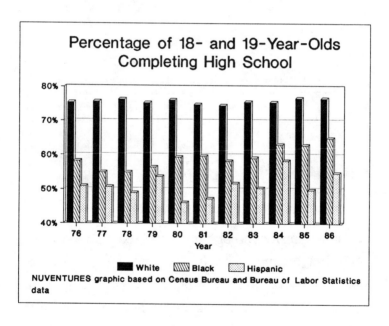

Percentage of 18- and 19-Year-Olds Completing High School

NUVENTURES graphic based on Census Bureau and Bureau of Labor Statistics data

At the college level, enrollment by Hispanic and Asian students increased somewhat in the early 1980s, but Black attendance dropped from 34% of those finishing high school in 1976 to 26% in 1985.[1]

During the 1990s, it must become a priority of the nation to improve the education of minorities, or we will increasingly become a nation of the "haves" and the "have nots."

The disparity between educational levels attained by minorities and those attained by Whites is one factor that has traditionally led to minorities being over represented in occupations with the least growth potential. Blacks and Hispanics are employed, to a larger extent than Whites, in occupations that require less education and training, have lower average earnings, and which are projected to grow at a slower rate.[2]

Unless improvements are made, a significant proportion of minorities will continually remain at a disadvantage in obtaining the best paying jobs and will have fewer opportunities in the future job market. The improvement needs to be more than cosmetic. We do not need large numbers of people pushed through an educational system just to bolster the graduation rate statistics.

What is needed is an upgrading of our educational system, coupled with Parental Reinforcement of the need to become educated.

Company Efforts to Improve Minority Education

Improving the educational achievement of minority students will require a concerted effort by government, business, parents, and the public.

Many companies have already funded and actively participated in programs that encourage minority students to stay in school. They have assisted public school systems in meeting the needs of minority children. For example:

♦ Los Angeles schools, in partnership with several employer foundations, have established a drop out prevention program. It targets students considered at risk of leaving school early. The program provides students with on and off campus social services to help address important nonacademic needs.[3]

♦ In Seattle, University Hospital employees and Hartford Insurance workers are pen pals with at-risk students in elementary schools.[4]

♦ A partnership including 40 local Los Angeles companies awards small grants to educators who utilize imagination and innovation in the classroom. Particular emphasis is placed on ventures that serve the needs of disadvantaged minority students.[5]

In the future, an increasing number of employers will sponsor programs that prepare students academically for college and emphasize basic skills needed to meet the demands of a changing workplace. Many of these projects will take the form of Public School Partnerships, where businesses provide students with educational resources (such as computers or laboratory equipment) and tutoring by professionals. Internships and work study programs will introduce students to corporate culture and expose them to the opportunities available, while emphasizing the value education plays in career advancement.

Companies will also play a larger role in funding college scholarships for children in need, especially those in inner-city neighborhoods.

Role Models

One of the most beneficial programs initiated by employers provides role models or mentors for minority students and employees. **More than almost any other source, role models can communicate the potential for success to both students and employees.** Successful minority executives can encourage students to get a good education and demonstrate the advantages of staying in school. The stories of how they succeeded provide memorable examples for students to follow.

Since the only "cost" of a role model program is the executives' time while they are involved in the project, even small companies can take part in this undertaking which shows students, by example, what the future could hold for them.

Mentor programs also provide role models for the company's employees. As part of these programs, a successful executive who is not their supervisor, counsels a worker, providing advice and guidance. Using mentors for new minority employees will help retain these workers and make sure that the firm is sensitive to their needs.

Employee Training

Because many new workers will not have the skills needed to meet complex job requirements, employers will be taking a more active training role. Businesses will teach employees basic math, reading, and language skills. In addition, new employees will be taught technical skills for entry level jobs and advanced skills to facilitate movement up the organizational hierarchy.

Training will be conducted by in-house personnel, as well as by outside centers sponsored in conjunction with community service groups and other businesses.

At the same time, executives and other company personnel will receive training in being responsive to a multicultural workforce.

Ensuring Opportunities for Advancement

To foster motivation and commitment among its workers, companies will be careful to have in place policies to ensure that all workers have equal opportunities for advancement.

Providing mentors to facilitate the entry of minorities into the workplace, help them feel comfortable, and assure that they express their ideas and that those ideas are acknowledged is one of the ways companies will secure the success of these workers. Mentors can also see that each employee has an opportunity to maximize his or her potential and advance in the company.

Minority workers achieving a good education to prepare them for the decade ahead will have at their disposal incredible opportunities for advancement. American companies will be actively seeking to employ minority employees with good skills.

TOMORROW'S TECHNOLOGICAL DEVELOPMENTS

♦ **The pace of the 1990s technological developments will be several times faster than that which we witnessed during the 1980s.**

♦ **New technologies will add millions of jobs during the 1990s but, in doing so, they will also eclipse many existing industries.**

♦ **Participants in the coming workforce will have to adapt successfully to an ever quickening pace of new technologies and challenges or be relegated to less responsible positions.**

♦ **Continual updating and reeducation on new equipment, technologies, and techniques will be a necessity for successful professionals and skilled technicians in every industry.**

As will be discussed in Chapter IX, of the 20 fastest growing occupations projected for the 1990s, about half of them will be associated with the medical field, and most of the rest will be computer related.

Biotechnology and Medicine

With the population getting older, we will need increased medical services. But more than being just market driven, the field of medicine is also undergoing a dramatic transformation because of rapidly advancing technological developments. These are replacing many traditional medical practices and tools.

Some of the new Biotechnology processes involve making basic changes in the genetic structures of simple microbes so they will react under certain conditions to produce desired products. Applications of Biotechnology in Medicine and other industries involve inserting new genes or gene blockers into living organisms with the goal of defeating hereditary diseases, forestalling aging, developing microbes to attack hazardous waste, or creating better livestock or food plants.

♦ In late 1989, scientists successfully identified the gene responsible for the occurrence of Cystic Fibrosis. Real hope now exists that scientists in the foreseeable future will be able to develop an antidote which either blocks the activity of that gene, or can find a way to biologically exclude it from developing cells.

♦ A number of important pharmaceuticals are now being produced using Biotechnology discoveries and techniques including: insulin, interferon, and the human growth factor (hGF).

New medicines will be made from biotechnological processes in every year of the 1990s, and at an ever quickening pace. Often this new generation of product will come from a totally new technological approach. **Each time these new medicines are produced, the replacement product will more often than not come from another company. This will cause a frequent shifting of jobs from one firm to another.** In a few cases the same company will make the new discovery, and people will simply begin working on a new product.

For the most part, Biotechnological production processes will require less space and cost. They will not require the huge start up manufacturing and construction costs of current manufacturing facilities. Many Biotechnology products will be made utilizing vats of fermenting organisms.

Potential controversy and distrust is inherent in any process which alters basic living structure A cottage industry will grow up around Biotechnology, to monitor its byproducts and to keep it from getting out of control.

Biotechnology discoveries are not only finding applications in medicine, but in food production, agriculture, and the design of new manufacturing processes.

Medical treatments of the 1990s will be faster and more routine than ever before, with patients needing to spend far less time in the hospital:

♦ One new development will be the use of lasers to weld tissue back together after a trauma. The process is called Tissue Anastomosis. All the future surgeon will have to do is tape the torn tissue to hold it in place during welding.[1] There is virtually no damage to the appearance of the tissue. The surgical tape is transparent to the wavelengths utilized.

Routinely, people will be able to monitor their own vital life signs. High blood pressure monitoring has been available to the general public since the late 1980s. Cholesterol, and other blood measurements will be regularly monitored at a company clinic for a fraction of their present costs. Companies will eagerly encourage their employees to submit to these health monitors.

As we learn more and more each year about the operations of the human body and what it requires to extend a healthy life, companies will increasingly be involved in sharing this knowledge through Wellness campaigns.

Computers - Smaller, Faster, and Verbal

Computers, especially the personal computer, led the vast technological developments of the 1980s. The rate of acceptance of personal computers during the past decade was dramatic:

♦ Commercially introduced in the mid-1970s, personal computers were used by only 7% of white collar workers in 1983. However, in 1986, 22% of white collar workers used personal computers, and a third used them in 1988. By 1991, it is estimated that 61% of these workers will utilize personal computers.[2]

Personal computers will continue to be in the forefront of the 1990s technological advance, primarily because they are so versatile and relatively inexpensive per unit. They are also capable of serving as a medium for utilizing many of the newest technologies, or as a linkage for several types of technologies and applications. As the size of microchips shrink, manufacturers will seek to put more and more components into smaller units, until eventually we have a unit capable of an immense number of tasks.

♦ This decade's computers will incorporate the technology of cellular telephones, FAX machines, copiers, optical scanners, and laser printers, all rolled into one package.

New breakthroughs will be rapidly decreasing the physical size and, at the same time, multiplying the performance capabilities of microprocessors. By the year 2000, the personal computer of 1990 will seem as limited in capability as the hand held calculators of the early

1970s seem today.

♦ Experimental computers have been developed which can actually read and interpret data. In the near future it is highly likely that computers will be able to intelligently search large data bases and to draw conclusions based upon what they find.[3]

Today's laptop computer will be large compared to tomorrow's standards. Wallet sized personal computers may become pencil thin and will be limited in their other dimensions by the physical size of the human hand and the space which fingers need to type information into a keyboard as efficiently as possible. For the near term, palm sized computers will serve many scheduling and other functions, except large scale word and data entry processing.

Touch screens will also become much more prevalent as a means to control the menus of small computer systems.

♦ Nynex has a computer enhanced phone system which will automatically dial phone numbers in a computer data base memory by just touching the name of the party you want called.

Personal computers will have brilliant full color Liquid Crystal Display (LCD) screens. Alternatively, where a finer screen definition is needed, today's standard Cathode Ray Tube will become high definition (more lines per screen) just as televisions have before them.

Compact disks, similar to those for recorded music today, will revolutionize data storage. Currently, a single compact disk can store the equivalent of 275,000 pages of text or 1,800 floppy disks,[4] and future technology will increase its storage capacity. Businesses will be able to greatly reduce the storage space needed for data and cut the cost of sending information to customers and suppliers. Furthermore, merchandise catalogs, parts lists, and government documents will become widely available on compact disks. Entire volumes of library data will be accessible on a single disk.

On the horizon, photons or light spectrum signals will be successfully harnessed to work many of our computers and other electronically powered systems. These optical computers will process data 1,000 to 10,000 times faster than current electronic computers.[5]

Semiconductors will be available in the mid 1990s which are 1/100 the size of today's versions, and which will work on quantum mechanic principals whereby electrons confined to tiny enclosures emit wave like behavior. Many fiber optic improvements will be able to augment these advances. Certain fiber optic devices can be made to switch or reverse the direction of light signals just as a transistor switches electrical currents based on voltage. Potentially these devices could process data thousands of times faster than today's computers.

♦ Fiber optic systems are about to be incorporated into certain aircraft designs so that light signals can be sent to wings, tail flaps and stabilizers without electrical interference that might result from random lightning strikes.[6]

Even smaller power sources will be able to drive these photon based systems and devices. For the first time true solar power will drive many computers and other devices with a completely independent source of power. This will free many new inventions for greater in-field applications where the absence of electricity has been a detriment. New solar power technologies will increase efficiencies for conversion to electrical power to above 25%.[7] This will be sufficient to bring this much desired technology into a number of realistic applications.

Talking to Computers

By the late 1990s, computers will be activated largely by voice commands. Already we see "talking" microchips everywhere, from point of purchase displays to dashboard systems, and some cellular phones can now be voice operated. At first these computer based mnemonics systems will only be able to be used to respond to limited verbal commands like "On, access directory x," etc. As output their first commands will include, "Wake up, you're late for your appointment," etc.

Eventually the ever increasing memory and speed of personal computers will allow us to dictate letters and see a printed version on the screen.

At first these dictated versions of letters will be only suitable for rough drafts, and will have to be corrected with a keyboard. In time, they will become more and more accurate.

When letters are sent by computer FAX (Email), the end user will have the choice of visually reading a letter on the screen or listening to their computer read it to them. For variety, eventual systems might feature the accent of the message writer or of a famous celebrity.

Language Translation

Hand held computers with voice synthesizers will be the language translators of the next century. Soon we will be able to speak into small units which translate the message into another language quite correctly within a matter of seconds.

Computer programs and equipment in existence in the early 1990s are the beacon of what is to come:

♦ One affordable series of programs from MicroTac of San Diego, California translates approximately a 30,000 word vocabulary and many irregular verbs into something very close to respectable Spanish, French, German, and Italian.

♦ The Voice Explorer by Advanced Products and Technology of Redmond, Washington utilizes a voice processor, microphone, and speaker to "converse" with the user. A translator converts words, phrases, or sentences in its 35,000 word dictionary from English to Spanish, French, or Japanese.[8]

Currently, users need to have a working knowledge of the language's grammar to make these programs work most effectively. But for now, programs with automatic replacement features, eliminate the tedium of looking up vocabulary in the dictionary. It is up to the end user to adjust the word order and select the correct irregular verb. Eventually, these types of programs will become increasingly "grammar smart" and very affordable.

These programs will allow international trading partners to communicate directly. For the first time in world history, any business person will be able to initiate a conversation with any other business person. A great period of new international business will lay the foundation for a very different 21st Century.

CAD/CAM

Revolutionizing the world of designing shoes, complex circuit boards, and just about everything in between will be CAD/CAM (Computer Aided Design/Computer Aided Manufacturing). Dedicated computers able to help design manufactured pieces of equipment became available by the mid 1980s. With the new power of personal computers, CAD/CAM programs are available which can run on the standard personal computers. They have or will soon revolutionize traditional engineer/draftsman teams, speed up the design process, and greatly lower the cost of design so that it can be accomplished in a small shop.

♦ Even at your local dentist, you will soon be able to see your current decaying tooth on a video image, and then be able to see it displayed in the manner it will appear after your Dentist has repaired it. And talk about the perfect crown, by the time that CAM is finished with defining all the contours and creases in the surface of your remaining tooth, you will never have a more perfect fit.[9]

CAD systems will allow the drawer to plot out his device, and then employ various criteria to make the design more efficient. As corrections are made, the program continually improves upon itself until the best design is achieved. CAM systems study the manufacturing specifications and will ultimately direct robot lathes to more efficiently shape products.

On the horizon are affordable "three dimensional printers" that create physical models from CAD/CAM designs. Current printers use lasers to fashion three dimensional models from photosensitive plastic, powders, or other materials, one layer at a time.[10] Eventually, designers will be able to fashion a new children's toy or some other object and have a physical model created in a matter of minutes. The ultimate goal is to have "desktop manufacturing" that will build prototypes and possibly even usable products.

Not only is CAD/CAM being used to design physical products, it is also utilized on an atomic scale by leading chemical and pharmaceutical companies to study the physical shapes and properties of molecules ranging from antibodies to genes. CAD/CAM programs can store data on the shapes and properties of millions of molecules which might be able to identify a proper molecular fit.

Using these programs scientists can eliminate much trial and error by designing theoretical molecular shapes on the computer which will block an active site. Not all theoretical designs will work in real life, but they measurably reduce the number of possibilities that need to be tested, while simultaneously giving scientists new insights into the operation of basic biochemical mechanisms.

Electronic Still Photography

Electronic still photography will be in full bloom by the mid 1990s. It was employed to a limited extent in disk cameras offered in the late 1980s, but its development has been inhibited by the limited memory of current devices. With the expected improvements in the memory capacity of computers by the end of the decade, computerized images will have completely replaced traditional silver film technology, except for some specialized uses of the professional photographer.

111

Electronic images can be instantaneously transmitted over telephone lines to other locations. The electronic pixel images will also be able to be manipulated on a computer. For example, an architect whose client wants to add a second story to a building can take its picture with an electronic camera. Then, the image can be transferred to a computer, where the first story can be copied to simulate a second story. Windows can be moved around, and even landscaping can be added.[11]

One major development of ESP will be the likely elimination of most uses for the traditional photocopier. Electronic scanners can scan documents and preserve them electronically. This will include all but formal legal documents (Wills, deeds, contracts, etc.). Most documents will remain on computerized memory where they can be found and accessed on the computer screen. Gone from the office will be the cumbersome filing cabinets and the frantic searches for a missing document.

Office Communications

Telephones will also undergo several technological improvements during the 1990s. The first will be Caller

ID where a person, before answering their phone call, will know the telephone identity of the caller. This will eliminate nuisance calls for many. The next changes will include further mobility around the office, with smaller and smaller cordless phones.

Fiber optic technology will make "picture telephones" common equipment of the future. Not only will they let workers see to whom they are talking, but picture telephones will also let skilled technicians in the office recommend field repairs by allowing them to see the problem in the field. Companies will be able to view a Paris fashion designer's new spring line or assess production modifications in a factory in Singapore. Conference calls will truly be conference calls as we see several people on a monitor, seemingly having a face to face discussion, while in reality, they will be talking from thousands of miles away.

Electronic Mail Systems

Companies are already placing less reliance on "traditional" mail and have increasingly turned to electronic mail for normal business to business communication.

♦ In each month of 1989, 31 million electronic mail messages were sent to 1.6 million electronic mailboxes.[12]

As one manager stated:

If we have to wait for the U.S. mail, it may be too late to take action in today's fast paced world. Hours count, not days.

Equipped with electronic mail technology, voice recognition programs, and voice synthesizers, personal computers will eliminate the need for most physical letters. Workers will be able to compose messages at their computers and send them electronically to anyone in their company or even to recipients all over the world. As voice recognition systems are developed, a person will be able to dictate a letter to the computer, even by telephone and callers will be able to telephone a computer to leave messages. The addition of voice synthesizers would let workers call their computer from any telephone and listen to written messages they have received.

Electronic mail systems will include search features to help organize and find messages so that an executive who today misplaces a message will be able to easily locate a record of his or her calls. There will also be security systems so that only the intended recipient can listen to the messages.

Location and Navigation

A growing network system of Transmission Data Relay Satellite Systems are changing overnight the way we identify the location of everything on earth. These TDRSS satellites are located in geosynchronous orbit 36,000 kilometers above the earth. They were placed into orbit at speeds which exactly match the rotating speed of the earth, but they orbit in the opposite direction ensuring that they maintain the same precise position relative to the earth's surface.

The advantage of TDRSS in a stationary orbit is that the satellites can return signals more precisely and with a far weaker signal than was necessary in the past when signaling Satellites were constantly changing their position relative to the earth's surface. These former systems had to allow for differences in the speed of returning signals relative to their own motion around the earth.

TDRSS reflected signals are so accurate that they allow receivers mounted on moving vehicles to identify exactly where on earth they are located. Their accuracy can be as precise as a few meters for military applications. These global positioning systems are also ensuring that future vehicles of all kinds can be equipped to always know their exact location. This includes not only boats, and airplanes, but also every day delivery and rescue vehicles.

Owners of large scale fleets can also utilize the system on a strategic scale to know exactly where every one of their vehicles is located.

♦ IImorrow, a United Parcel Service (UPS) company, has one such system in operation which can display to management exactly where every one of its parent company's UPS delivery trucks is located. The CRT display can portray an entire city scale or zoom down into a neighborhood to observe the exact location of every one of its trucks on a video map of that city's streets. In the street by street mode they can observe small rectangles with identifying numerical codes as they move down city streets.

♦ The same company has a similar system in place for the Detroit, Michigan and Portland, Oregon police departments. From a monitoring location they can see where every patrol car is and observe every street where they may be moving or stopped. Five patrol cars linked together may mean a serious incident or the location of the best coffee shop in town. When a dispatcher needs to send a second vehicle to another's assistance, they can observe its progress while driving enroute to that location. They can even give the driver directions to take the next right or left if necessary. These prototype systems will be commonplace by the mid 1990s.

Tracking systems have long been in operation for the commercial airlines, but will now be made incredibly more accurate by TDRSS enhanced information. Commercial airlines will be able to observe where all of its planes are on a worldwide scale. One color indicates planes are on the ground, another that they are in flight. The latter move across graphic country or world maps to reflect their changing latitude and longitude. Other symbols indicate that a vehicle is late, and will highlight all connecting flights to be affected by the delay of that one plane. A computer system will recommend alternatives to a master scheduler so that certain flights schedules be adjusted to maximize customer flow. Passengers with special connection problems will be handed a customized adjusted schedule while they are still on board the arriving aircraft. They will be allowed to call affected persons via cellular phone.

♦ By the mid 1990s salespersons making calls, trucks making deliveries, or rental car customers will be able to consult with a computer scheduler which reads their present position and displays it in the midst of a graphic map. A Zip+4 code or other destination ID will be sufficient to recommend a travel route on the map and be able to highlight directions to the destination. If several stops are required, as in deliveries, the vehicular navigation system will be able to recommend the most efficient routing using mathematical operations research algorithms. Later systems will also be able to incorporate on time information about current traffic flow on major highways and be able to incorporate this into a suggested route.

In a nutshell, we will be able to get anywhere we want to go faster, sooner, and with less cost. However, employers purchasing these systems will require that they be utilized to increase the number of deliveries or sales calls per day. To do less would be inefficient, and would ultimately hurt their competitiveness.

More, not less, will be expected from those given more powerful technological tools with which to operate. Intense competition from overseas and domestic competitors will not allow the American worker an easier day. It will instead require that each worker be more productive and efficient.

Robotics

Robots will take over more and more of the routine functions in our home, office, factory, and laboratory. Most of these devices will not yet be the walking Bipeds of science fiction stories. They will instead be a single purpose machine combined with a computer brain. Most of them will have artificial intelligence capability and will rely on "what if" logic, or ambient signals to trigger activity. Some applications we will see in our future work place before the end of the next decade will be:

♦ At night a robot vacuum cleaner will follow a programmed pattern to clean the office, saving considerable cleaning costs. Waste baskets would now be adapted so that the robot can take their contents away. Similar systems will be used by Lawn Maintenance firms to cut grass and collect debris on customers' lawns eliminating expensive manpower.

♦ Robots will routinely divide animal carcasses into precise cuts of meat, which are then automatically packaged. A technician will supervise the operation of several of these mechanical butchers, who will be able to out produce 200 of their human counterparts.

♦ An elaborate security system will operate within certain sections of companies and homes. There will be optical recognition of thumbprint to gain admittance, followed by a voice confirmation from the entrant. Illegal break-ins will be detected by a sentry robot, and the police will be summoned immediately.

♦ Visual recognition capabilities of robots will allow them to scan thousands of manufactured parts per hour and to eliminate those not conforming to specifications. This will create excellent quality control over manufactured products.

♦ Future fast food stores will eliminate human order takers, to allow their customers to select meals by pressing a button, and then inserting their bank card into a slot prior to receiving their food, which will have just been prepared by robot chefs who are supervised by a human technician. The food they produce will be flawlessly prepared, cooking oils will be changed according to specification, and the highest standards of cleanliness will be maintained.

Robots already automatically weld ship hulls and aircraft fuselages at companies like General Dynamics and Rohr. In the 1990s they will be utilized more and more to perform important, but routine and monotonous jobs now being performed by humans.

Technological innovations will be a major factor contributing to the decreased proportion of new low level jobs available in the 1990s.

Entertainment/Training

Entertainment will be more and more participatory by the turn of the century. Video games being released in the early 1990s allow the participant to run, or conduct movements which are replicated by a representative figure on the screen. By the late 1990s similar devices will be utilized to supplement all types of training requiring hands on interaction. Eventually giant wrap around screens with high definition will let us visualize that we are in exotic settings soaking up the sun, rather than just lounging in a play room.

Within two decades holography will allow the participant to visualize that they are really on a ski slope, flying a space shuttle, or reliving a frontal assault on Omaha beach. Management scenarios will follow, where the computer based opponents act and react with us in a rather human fashion, when they do not get their way.

Future training will become very participatory.

CHAPTER VII

THE FUTURE WORKPLACE

- ♦ **By the year 2000, ninety percent of today's "paperwork" will be electronic.** There will be virtually no conventional filing cabinets in offices. Office designs will strive for spacious elegance.

- ♦ **Increasingly companies will want to monitor the health of their workers,** and counsel them on proper activities to maximize their own as well as their family's health. They will simultaneously monitor workers for drug, alcohol, and other abuses.

- ♦ Because of the increasingly short market life of new products, **companies will employ tough new security technologies to insure that their products, and ideas are not stolen.**

- ♦ **The business office will remain the principal American workplace. Only a small proportion of the American workforce will work from their home on a full time basis.**

The New Workplace

By the end of the 1990s, ninety percent of "paperwork" output will be electronic.

♦ Gone from many offices will be the rows of filing cabinets housing corporate files. One or two filing cabinets will house important paper documents. Virtually all files within will have an electronic counterpart.

♦ Frantic searches to locate missing documents will be a thing of the past. As long as a document was properly saved, search commands will not only find items, but bring them up on a screen.

People will still sit in chairs at desks. But the emphasis of the future office will be to provide the illusion of spaciousness. Computer terminals will take up less space than they do now. New office buildings constructed during the 1990s will try to provide a sense of space by designing wall voids as places to house electronic storage. They will incorporate shielding impervious to destructive magnetic influences.

Offices will also feature areas where large size viewing screens can be observed by a group of people in meetings. Offices will be equipped with large viewing screens for the frequent educational and training programs which will become a more frequent ingredient of the business environment. Projectors and transparencies will be a relic of the past.

Traditional Japanese architecture with its themes of simplicity and openness will flourish in future business motifs. Office design will emphasize setting a mood which is soothing, but commensurate with progress. In the high tech office there will be an emphasis placed on contrasting natural adornments like live plants and trees. At larger companies, space will be set aside for relaxation and exercise.

Learn or Step Aside

Just about anyone who buys electronic equipment, even a video cassette recorder or a compact disc player, understands that you do not simply open the package and start using the item. Just about every computer, software, and printer available requires some minimum number of hours for installation, and linkage between the various hardware and software components to be utilized.

After installation there is a learning period of from one hour to several days to get most applications running smoothly. During the time that a good piece of hardware or software is used, there are frequently several hours a month invested in looking up and experimenting with the nuances of its use.

One key essential of working with any of the new technologies is the need to be able to read and comprehend complex directions in order to be able to install, program, or work with these devices. Even though video training programs will be available to assist in using many devices, having a good vocabulary, reasoning skills, and math ability will be a necessity to function effectively in the 1990s. **There will be so much to learn in managing and working with high technology devices, that those with polished learning skills at every level from management to factory worker will have a clear and decisive advantage.**

As was elaborated upon in our Education section, many of our high school graduates of today are not educationally equipped to start up and begin running most pieces of business software, even those which are "user friendly." The vocabulary needed to understand some of the terms demands that the user have the desire to explore and learn.

♦ Words like kerning, array, cropping, matrix, function, ordinate, icon, font, macro, and justify, are all common terms used to describe routine software manipulations today.

In the rapidly advancing technological atmosphere of the 1990s, those with an insufficient vocabulary and underdeveloped reasoning skills are going to find it increasingly more difficult to obtain success from their jobs. Those unable to adapt to a faster and faster pace of technology will find their careers eclipsed as they are relegated into less important roles.

For those hoping to derive more than just a paycheck from their job in the 1990s, the marching order will be "Learn, or step aside."

Health Monitoring

Considerable technology to monitor our vital life signs is already in place and will be dramatically increasing in capability during the 1990s. The monitoring of human biological functions will be declining in cost and in complexity. **Many employers will use routine health monitoring by company clinics as a means of cutting soaring health care insurance costs. In addition it will provide employees with an early warning of possible danger to their health.**

Employers will seek to submit employees to tests to monitor blood, and respiratory, and other health signs. This will be accomplished at the office, on a short turn around time table.

♦ The positive side of this will be people will have an early warning of potential problems like high blood pressure, cancer, diabetes, etc.

Because of the concerns about illegal drug use and alcohol abuse, most new employees of the nineties will have to submit to tests for these substances. Upon hiring they will have to agree, as a condition of employment, to submit to periodic health testing. Employees found abusing their bodies will be asked to submit to prescribed therapy or be terminated.

Companies will improve the ambient office and factory environments because the new medical monitoring will help detect potential occupational hazards sooner than ever before. There will be many cases of companies finding out through their own monitoring that they are having a deleterious impact on their workers' health.

Stress and its damaging effects will motivate a whole new body of research on how to best get employees to fulfill their maximum potential without damaging their health. As a result, companies will pay a lot of attention to environment, atmosphere, and exercise.

Security

The potential for crime around the immediate working environment of the 1990s will be greater than ever before:

♦ The Drug problem.

♦ An older workforce which would be more prone to become victims of crime.

These factors will motivate companies to increase security around Corporate offices, warehouses, and other property. Computers and robots are perfect devices to help provide security.

In the future, surveillance devices will not only allow security people to view remote locations, but they will routinely electronically photograph facilities and store the surveillance data for later use.

Thumbprint readers, which work like bar code readers at the supermarket, will be used to monitor passage through facilities. Computers will store information about who passed through every door and when. Unusual patterns of movement will be identified by computers and brought to the attention of security personnel.

Detectors will be commonplace to sense what is being carried in or out of offices. Especially important will be devices to sense the transportation of magnetic disks and other devices. Otherwise, a great deal could be stolen in a coat pocket filled with valuable disks or chips. Companies with heavy investments in R&D or design will commonly scan all employees entering or leaving. Security personnel alerted to these movements will ask targeted employees to open their briefcases, pocket books, etc. as companies try to protect their investment.

The need for security will result in the monitoring of telephone lines for FAX or modem signals to identify whether or not the transmissions are in the company's interests. These security procedures will be unknown to most employees. Emergency procedures will be available to stop unwanted transmissions and to destroy the portions already at the receiving location. Computer systems will be able to read and identify unwanted transmissions within moments.

Companies will be especially concerned with security because of the increasingly short market life of many new products. Firms will find that getting a product enhancement on the market first will be a tremendous strategic marketing advantage.

Repair It Yourself

For some time now, it has been more economical for a company to replace, rather than repair, much of its broken office equipment.

♦ A couple of years ago, a small company received an erroneous signal on a computer screen when one of the letter keys of the brand name keyboard was pressed. They temporarily exchanged keyboards from another unit and discovered that the problem was indeed coming from the keyboard itself.

The major computer manufacturer was called to get service. The small company did not have a service contract. They were told that it would cost $175 for the first hour of a serviceman's visit, and of course there would be no guarantee that he could repair the equipment in that time period.

They delayed the service visit, and decided to find out what it would cost to replace the unit. After twenty minutes of telephone calling, a new keyboard was found for approximately $90. It was still functioning in their office two years later.

Similarly, the job of service and repair of all items is increasingly going to become throw away, because the cost of mass produced replacement modules is declining so rapidly.

♦ There is a Korean multinational electronics manufacturer called Goldstar who imports over one million 12" color CRT units (just the screen) into the United States annually for use as components of various devices. In quantity the cost of production is only approximately $12 per unit. With high labor costs, in the U.S., it is far cheaper to throw away a defective screen, than have someone try and repair it.

In many cases, office workers are going to be performing their own repairs rather than waiting for service to come to them.

♦ Many software programs have a hardware component. They are supplied with instructions on how to open up the personal computer in order to install the FAX, modem, scanner, or mouse hardware. These installation instructions usually include a warning that the installer needs to be careful about possibly voiding the manufacturer's warranty if they open up the personal computer. But with the cost of many personal computers plummeting, the time saved is of much more value than a warranty.

♦ In 1985, it would have been unheard of to open up a personal computer yourself. By the early 1990s, many of us will have become used to it. Rather than having to take the unit over to expensive and time consuming repair facilities, the worker will just insert a replacement module. For years, consumers have been plugging telephone equipment in and out, after the basic lead wiring has been installed.

Copying machines, a necessity in the office environment, are becoming smaller and less expensive. And as forecast in the previous chapter, they will tend to become eclipsed by Electronic Still Photography by the late 1990s.

In larger office environments there will likely be an additional staff member who becomes the "repair wizard," but who, in reality, usually only removes covers and changes modules.

Machines of the 1990s will be designed to identify which specific part is causing the error and needs replacement.

Bar codes will very likely find their way onto the millions of different parts so that a repair person can scan quickly the item needing repair and then send the scanned image over the FAX to a central ordering point which can then arrange next day delivery of the suspect part.

The Salesperson of the 1990s

During the 1990s, the salesperson's personal computer and car will be an office on the move. While visiting a client, the salesperson may place an order on the spot by FAX using a laptop or palm sized computer. By calling the factory, warehouse, or home office computer, product availability can be checked, and the customer can select substitute products if necessary. Confirmation of the order will be sent via FAX to the customer. Or instead, the salesperson may send the order and receive confirmation with the laptop computer and cellular telephone in his or her car.

Messages, industry news, additional information on customers, credit ratings, and price changes will also be available electronically. Important messages will be sent or received from the car via FAX if a hard copy is needed.

The salesperson will use their computer by talking to it, making driving time more productive. For example, the salesperson can tell the computer to call the next customer, and that person's number will be dialed so the appointment can be confirmed. The salesperson will be able to dictate personalized promotional literature for the next customer and have a professional quality printout before he or she arrives at the location.

The computer will determine the most efficient route to cover a territory. The salesperson will program into the computer the locations that must be visited, and the course that minimizes travel time will be planned. Furthermore, a detailed computerized map will indicate the specific roads to take to the next client's location. The driver will also be alerted to any conditions that may cause delays, such as an accident tying up traffic, and alternate routes will be suggested.

Future of the Office at Home

There has been much discussion about whether or not a substantial number of employees will find that they will be working out of their homes by the turn of the century. One of the leading Human Resource managers expressed the prevailing opinion among large corporate personnel experts:

I can't see it happening on a large scale for big corporations. People need to interact to address problems and to come up with the best ideas. Someone working out of the home would be out of touch as far as strategic thinking goes. They would miss the major decisions made in the office every day. They would find it difficult to advance; out of sight, out of mind.

Another said:

We have experimented with allowing some women with children to work out of the home and the efficiencies have been terrible. The only possible way to do it is on a piece rate basis. Very few of the people we would consider trusting to work out of their home would be working on something which could be done on a piece rate basis.

Many leading executives use their portable computers to occasionally work from home if they are sick, or about to travel and want to keep frequent contact with the office. Occasionally, they also report working from home for variety.

However, many working at home reported problems with concentration, and the distraction of children or a nearby refrigerator. Most agreed it was not an easy task to get work accomplished at home on a regular basis.

The home office will likely remain the domain of only a relatively few situations:

- **Very small, local service companies.**

- **Second career, retired executives.**

- **People in lone creative occupations, such as writing, consulting, design, art, etc.**

- Salespeople or servicepeople handling a local territory for a nationwide company.

Even though other types of jobs could be done at home with advancing technology, companies will favor having employees interact with each other in the business workplace.

THE CHANGING SHAPE OF U.S. BUSINESS

♦ Immediately after World War II, the United States represented nearly half of the Gross National Product of the entire World. **By the beginning of the 21st Century, the U.S. will represent only a little more than one fifth of the world's economic power.**

♦ Technological efficiencies will allow smaller companies, to perform the role which once only very large companies could fulfill. **During the 1990s, the majority of new jobs will be added by companies employing 50 to 250 people.**

♦ **High technology will cause many product life cycles to be less than three years.** Many smaller companies lacking the ability to repeat successes in a rapidly changing environment will fail. The rate of business failures will increase dramatically during the 1990s.

♦ **Unions have declined to the point where their membership now represents less than 17% of the total American workforce. By the year 2000, some forecast it will decline to 10%.**

Declining American Dominance

In 1950, the U.S. economy represented approximately 47% of the World's Gross National Product. During the 1980s, the nation's share of the World's Gross National Product had fallen to around one quarter of the world's total.[1] **By the year 2000, it will decline to approximately 22%,** as new economic centers continue to develop all over the world at a faster pace than the U.S. economy:

♦ The European Common Market will drop all internal trade barriers to become the second largest unified world market in 1992. (The 12 EEC countries had a combined Gross National Product equal to 62% of the United States GNP in 1985.)[2]

♦ The Eastern European countries, with opening markets, will begin to exert their own economic power by the turn of the century.

♦ In addition to Japan, several other Pacific rim countries are emerging as economic powers in their own right, especially Korea, Taiwan, Singapore, Australia, and others.

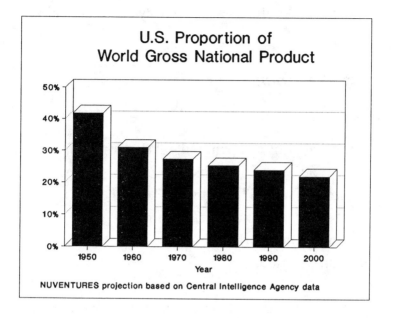

U.S. Proportion of
World Gross National Product

NUVENTURES projection based on Central Intelligence Agency data

America will no longer have as many of the world's leading corporations headquartered within her boundaries. Already, the largest U.S. Bank, Citicorp, is only ranked 27th in the world, based on deposits.[3] Over two decades ago, a majority of the world's largest banks were American.

As we enter a more global economy, and as America's share of the world economy continues to shrink, U.S. workers will have to become more accustomed to working under the management style of other cultures.

Smaller Companies will
Increase in Importance

The number of companies of all sizes operating in the United States will have increased from approximately 5.9 million in 1987 to roughly 7.0 million in the year 2000. The total number of people they employ will increase from nearly 125 million to 141 million during the same period.

However, there will be a considerable downward shift in the average size of firms. As shown in the accompanying table, the proportion of employees working for firms with 250 or more people will be declining during the 1990s, while the number of workers employed by companies with 50 to 250 people will increase dramatically.

One of the major driving forces behind this trend will be the high rate of technological advancement which is revolutionizing world business.

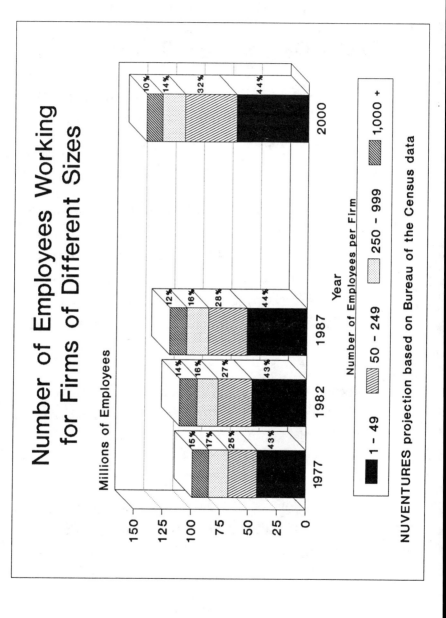

Number of Employees Working
for Firms of Different Sizes

Millions of Employees

Year	1 – 49	50 – 249	250 – 999	1,000 +
1977	43%	25%	17%	15%
1982	43%	27%	16%	14%
1987	44%	28%	16%	12%
2000	44%	32%	14%	10%

Number of Employees per Firm

■ 1 – 49   ▨ 50 – 249   ░ 250 – 999   ▧ 1,000 +

NUVENTURES projection based on Bureau of the Census data

Smaller Companies will Do More

One of the consequences of the new technologies will be that smaller sized companies will increasingly be able to do that which, before, only larger companies could accomplish.

♦ **Publishing** once required hundreds of thousands of dollars in typesetting, and camera equipment, and a large staff in art and other departments. This left the industry strictly in the domain of fairly large companies. Now with the desktop publishing software available for personal computers, the investment is far less.

♦ **Record production** once took full orchestras and accompaniment, but now music synthesizers can provide background music.

♦ **Product design** no longer requires a large group of people. Now, one hardworking person with a good CAD/CAM program can design a dress, a plumbing fixture, or a circuit board. After design, the engineer can readily find a small company to manufacture the product by searching computer data bases listing those with the capability to manufacture certain items. Soon "printers" will be able to construct replicas of product designs.

♦ **Biological research laboratories,** with a handful of people, can order from outside vendors a very specific, complex molecular sequence, on which they can conduct experimentation. This allows just a handful of scientists to perform research which before required a laboratory staffed by hundreds.

Having less overhead, smaller companies will be able to produce goods and services less expensively than larger companies. This phenomenon is the result of the new technological tools which carry a greatly reduced price tag. It has driven many large companies to trim layers of middle management in order to be able to compete with smaller competitors.

But small companies by virtue of their size and limited capital, are going to be more vulnerable than the larger companies which they are replacing.

Short Life of Products,
More Turnover of Companies

Because of the rapidly advancing pace of technology, products must be continually updated and improved. Think of how often your word processing or spread sheet software has changed over the past few years. We are constantly receiving new updates to replace the old.

♦ In today's high tech society a manufacturer is exceedingly fortunate if they can design a product which has a three year market life. They have to recoup their investment quickly. In computer or computer assisted products, the shelf life is even shorter. It's not long before another manufacturer is out with a better product.

Gone are the days when one great invention could be the basis of a company's success as Nylon was for DuPont, or the Safety Razor was for Gillette. Now a company has to continually make updates and enhancements to products even before the original product is on the market.

Some companies are not going to be successful at making the technological transition to the next generation of products. They will find themselves unable to compete, because there will be a greater proportion of smaller companies running the economy in the future. Many are going to be one or two product companies without the advantage of a wide repertoire of products to buoy them up if one fails. These smaller companies will also not possess the marketing expertise of their larger competitors.

A greater proportion of companies will fail in the 1990s than in any decade since the Great Depression. The ramifications of these business failures are already being felt within the investment community. Some workers will find that they will have to change employers several times during the nineties because their employer's business has failed.

Geographic Shifts

The sun belt states of the southwest and Florida will continue to be among the top geographic areas adding the most jobs during the 1990s.[4]

However, because of the aging of our workforce and the improvement in social conditions in many established communities, it will be unlikely that the 1990s migration levels will be as high as in past decades. In spite of this, one counter trend will be the increased use of nationwide call centers.

Consolidation into Nationwide Call Centers

During the late 1980s, nationwide operations began to centralize sales and, especially, service centers which answer "800" telephone numbers. From a centralized center, companies could better ensure that standardized procedures were followed and that critical supply shortfalls in one area could be filled promptly from excess supplies at another location.

Very often, these nationwide centers are located in less populous locations, often in the Midwest. The Midwest is favored because it is in the central time zone, and because the cost of living is frequently lower in small communities.

When a customer calls for service, he or she is simply asked for their Zip Code. That is how the caller can usually tell they are being serviced by a nationwide center.

♦ One system currently uses a local telephone number which makes the customer believe that they are receiving local service. In reality this number is being redirected to a nationwide call center.

The primary efficiency of a centralized center for calling in orders, service requests, etc. has been the ability to save manpower costs at many branch offices across the nation. More and more companies will find that the establishment of nationwide centers allows them to better manage their operations on a nationwide scale. They will also save tremendous costs by being able to trim back on local offices. In many cases, their local representative will work out of their own home, supported by a stipend to pay for the use of their facilities. The only link to the office will be a computer modem, or Email.

A secondary benefit is to ensure that company procedures are being followed to the letter, and a third is to be able to test on a daily basis responses to nation-wide or local advertising expenditures, etc.

Based on the number of enquiries related to an advertising theme, and questions asked in a subsequent survey, nationwide advertisers can measure responses with an accuracy level never before realized. More and more, nationwide centers will dominate the pattern of American business in the 1990s.

In the future these nationwide centers will become more high tech and an increasing proportion of the workforce will be employed by them. When service is necessary, the centralized center will provide the local service or salesperson with a daily schedule of stops, using a combination of customer priorities and operations research algorithms. As part of these computer based systems, the local representative will even be provided with directions. After a stop has been completed, the serviceperson will send in a brief status report indicating that the job has been completed, how much time it took, and which parts were used to make the repair. For a sales call, this can be a list of items which were ordered.

In many cases, the nationwide center will be able to track the vehicle using a Global Positioning System as described in the previous chapter.

♦ Companies with established nationwide centers include 3M, Xerox, Terminix, American Home Shield, United Airlines, and many others.

The Fate of Unionism

Despite reports by the Bureau of Labor Statistics which in 1988 showed that overall union members fared substantially better in respect to weekly wages ($480 per week) than their nonunion counterparts ($356 per week), the number of union members decreased from 20 million in 1980 to 17 million in 1984.[5]

The *number* of union members has remained virtually unchanged during the late 1980s, but the *proportion* of unionized workers declined. Eighteen percent of the workforce was unionized in 1985; by 1988 it was 16.8%.[6]

Factors contributing to this overall decline of unionism in America include the following:

- For the past 10 years, those sectors of the workforce which have traditionally been heavily organized, i.e. manufacturing, construction, and mining, have seen significant job losses due to international competition and automation. For example, the United Auto Workers Union lost 270 thousand jobs between the years of 1978 and 1988.[7]

- Manufacturing centers relocated from highly unionized areas in the Northeast and Great Lakes to the Sunbelt.

- The number of part time, short term workers, who are less likely to join unions, increased.

- Foreign owned, nonunion corporations operating in the U.S. increased.

- Much of the general population feels that unions are now obsolete. These workers feel that government legislation, and affirmative action programs, adequately protect them.

- An undercurrent of sentiment exists among many nonunion workers, that unions do not fully meet the needs and wants of their members. They also feel that members must settle for decisions in which they had little influence. This perception is particularly strong among working youth.[8]

As a result, the nation's unions appear that they will continue to decline. Industrial observers have forecast that the proportion of workers represented by unions will fall to as low as 10% of the overall workforce by the year 2000.[9]

The ultimate fate of unions will be based upon their ability to fulfill a need for individuals within industries where they have not been previously represented.[10]

One way unions are reaching a larger proportion of the workforce is through Associate Memberships. This type of membership extends various union benefits to workers who cannot be covered by union contracts. Associate members do not pay full dues as they do not receive the benefits of collective bargaining services.

♦ In 1988, approximately 2.2 million workers were represented by unions through Associate Memberships.[11]

Certain key employee groups will be targeted by unions for membership drives during the 1990s.

♦ **Women** - In 1988 women accounted for approximately 36% of all union members and recent research suggests that women show more interest in union membership than men.[12] With women expected to become a larger proportion of the future workforce, unions have targeted them as a key source of potential new members. Now more than ever, issues such as child care, parental leave, flexible scheduling, etc. are appearing on union agendas.

♦ **Minorities** - Of the additions to the workforce during the 1990s, minorities will represent 61%.

♦ **Professionals & Semi-Professionals** - Current labor law defines employees as either "workers" or "managers" and allows union representation of only those employees categorized as "workers."[13] Unions will be fighting to obtain new legal definitions so that they can better organize large semi-professional worker pools in the finance, trade, and other industries. These occupations have grown significantly over the past 10 years, or are projected to grow in the future.

Unions will also be preparing new agendas or issues for the 1990s to better appeal to the needs of the changing workforce. Some of the main provisions that will be stressed at the bargaining table include the following:

♦ **Education and Training** - Unions have structured education and job training programs to enable workers to more easily make transfers within a company. This also protects workers whose positions have a high likelihood of becoming obsolete.

♦ **Consideration of the two income family and single parents.** Needs for adequate child care, and leaves that do not penalize parenthood have increased.

♦ **Affordable comprehensive health care** including elder care. Unions are actively campaigning for some type of national health care program.

♦ **Negotiation for more labor-management committees** to put more responsibility into the hands of the workers. The objective is to help increase commitment and thereby increase production and product quality.

♦ **Equal pay and employment opportunities** regardless of race, gender and ethnicity.

♦ **Information, training, and equipment to deal with workplace hazards and to ensure safe work environments for employees.**

♦ **Minimum wage increases.**

The emerging global economy, effective legislative protections already in place, and more education required for new jobs are making the task of organizing workers more and more difficult. Unions are going to have to become more innovative and flexible in identifying the needs of those they wish to serve. Many believe that unions will not be able to make this transition.

CHAPTER IX

OCCUPATIONAL SHIFTS

♦ Between now and the year 2000, **half of the 20 fastest growing occupations will be in health services.** Most of the others will be computer related.

♦ **The occupation with the most rapid growth during the decade will be the paralegal profession.**

♦ **More workers will become retail salespersons** than will join any other vocation.

♦ By the year 2000, this nation's offices will employ **61,000 fewer typists,** and factories will utilize **170,000 less machine setters/operators. Farm workers will decrease by 153,000.**

Fastest Growing Occupations

Mirroring a rapid expansion of the legal profession (the number of lawyers will increase 31%) and a shifting of responsibilities within the legal community, **the number of paralegals will experience a phenomenal 75% growth between 1988 and the year 2000.**

Seven of the next eight fastest increasing vocations will be in health services. Jobs for medical assistants, home health aides, radiologic technologists, and medical records technicians will increase by 60% to 70%. Expansion of doctors' offices, group medical practices, health maintenance organizations, and other health care facilities will create strong demand for medical assistants and medical records technicians. At the same time, more of our population will be older and need medical care at home. Thus, there will be strong demand for home health aides. Radiation technology and ultrasound will play an even greater role in the diagnosis and treatment of diseases, so prospects for radiologic technicians are excellent.

Jobs for medical secretaries, physical therapists, and surgical technologists will also increase substantially.

Occupations related to computer technology will grow very rapidly. As businesses add more computers and as their existing equipment ages, the demand for people to repair this equipment (replace modules) will increase. Operations research analysts, who improve operating efficiency of all types of businesses, will have 55% more jobs available by the year 2000. Also, the market for computer systems analysts and computer programmers will be very strong.

Rapid growth will be experienced among salespersons in securities and financial services as well as travel agencies. The number of corrections officers and jailers will also greatly increase.

Other occupations with robust growth projections include electrical engineers, receptionists, and registered Nurses.

The twenty fastest growing occupations during the 1990s are listed in table on the following page.

TWENTY FASTEST-GROWING OCCUPATIONS

Occupation	Percent Change
Paralegals	75%
Medical Assistants	70%
Home Health Aides	68%
Radiologic Technicians and Technologists	66%
Data Processing Equipment Repairers	61%
Medical Records Technicians	60%
Medical Secretaries	58%
Physical Therapists	57%
Surgical Technologists	56%
Operations Research Analysts	55%
Securities and Financial Services Salespersons	55%
Travel Agents	54%
Computer Systems Analysts	53%
Physical and Corrective Therapy Assistants	53%
Social Welfare Service Aides	52%
Occupational Therapists	49%
Computer Programmers	48%
Human Services Workers	45%
Respiratory Therapists	41%
Corrections Officers and Jailers	41%

Source: Bureau of Labor Statistics

Technical Occupations

Computer related jobs and most engineering fields will experience sizable increases. Almost 260,000 new jobs for computer/math/operations research analysts and 250,000 new jobs for computer programmers will be created by the year 2000. More than 90,000 additional computer operators will be needed.

Openings for electrical engineers will increase by 176,000 because of strong demand for computers, electronic consumer goods, and communications equipment.

The market for data processing equipment repairers will increase by 44,000 jobs, but since few people have been in this profession, this represents a growth rate of 61% over 1988 levels.

Prospects for biologists, chemists, and chemical engineers will be more limited. Increased worker productivity and centralization of research will restrain growth in these vocations.

The following table gives the growth of selected technical occupations through the year 2000. Jobs are ranked by the change in number of employees. However, because some vocations currently have relatively few workers, occupations having small increases in the number of employees can have large growth rates (indicated by the percent change).

PROJECTED GROWTH TO 2000 FOR TECHNICAL OCCUPATIONS

Occupation	Number of Employees in 2000 (Thousands)	Change in Employees (1988-2000) (Thousands)	Percent Change (1988-2000)
Computer/Math/OR			
Analysts	763	259	52%
Computer Programmers	769	250	48%
Electrical Engineers	615	176	40%
Computer Operators	408	92	29%
Electronic Equipment			
Installers/Repairers	586	53	10%
Mechanical Engineers	269	44	20%
Data Processing			
Equipment Repairers	115	44	61%
Civil Engineers	219	32	17%
Biologists	72	15	26%
Chemists	93	13	17%
Chemical Engineers	57	8	16%

Source: Bureau of Labor Statistics

Professional Occupations

Protective service employees, teachers, child care workers, and accountants will multiply. More than 200,000 openings for security guards, accountants, secondary school teachers, and kindergarten and elementary school teachers will develop. Increasing crime will spur the demand for security guards, as well as for corrections officers and police officers. As the number of businesses grows, more accountants will be needed.

School enrollments will decline, but reductions in class sizes and continuing teacher turnover will add to the demand for teachers.

Population growth and business expansion will increase the market for legal services, so more than 180,000 openings for lawyers and more than 60,000 openings for legal secretaries and for paralegals will be generated.

Expanding numbers of working parents will add 186,000 jobs for child care workers.

On the other hand, the number of college faculty will change very little as college enrollments peak in the early 1990s.

Projected growth for many professional occupations is on the table on the following page.

PROJECTED GROWTH TO 2000 FOR PROFESSIONAL OCCUPATIONS

Occupation	Number of Employees in 2000 (Thousands)	Change in Employees (1988-2000) (Thousands)	Percent Change (1988-2000)
Security Guards	1,050	256	32%
Secondary Sch. Teachers	1,388	224	19%
Accountants	1,174	211	22%
Kindergarten/Elementary Teachers	1,567	208	15%
Child Care Workers	856	186	28%
Lawyers	763	181	31%
Financial Managers	802	130	19%
Police/Detectives	583	68	13%
Legal Secretaries	329	67	25%
Paralegals	145	62	75%
Personnel Specialists	305	53	21%
Aircraft Pilots	108	26	31%
Firefighters	257	24	10%
College Faculty	869	23	3%
Architects	107	21	25%
Economists	45	10	27%

Source: Bureau of Labor Statistics

Office Occupations

Jobs for office workers will be affected by technological improvements and by the decline of industries such as manufacturing.

New businesses will be established by men and women entrepreneurs, mature workers wanting to start "second" careers, and small companies with technology that enables them to do what only large firms previously could accomplish. New businesses will create many jobs for general managers, secretaries, receptionists, and office clerks, even though office technology will slow the rate of growth.

However, these increases will vary from industry to industry. For example, although there will be 385,000 more secretaries, the number employed by manufacturers and mining companies will decrease by 44,000.

PROJECTED GROWTH TO 2000 FOR OFFICE OCCUPATIONS

Occupation	Number of Employees in 2000 (Thousands)	Change in Employees (1988-2000) (Thousands)	Percent Change (1988-2000)
General Managers/Top Executives	3,509	479	16%
General Office Clerks	2,974	455	18%
Secretaries, except Legal/ Medical	3,288	385	13%
Receptionists	1,164	331	40%
Stockroom Clerks	841	63	8%
Telephone Operators	378	49	15%
File Clerks	290	27	10%
Bookkeeping/Accounting Clerks	2,272	20	1%
Data Entry Keyers	410	−21	−5%
Typists	924	−61	−6%

Source: Bureau of Labor Statistics

Computers in the office will limit the growth of some jobs and lead to a decline in others. Because much of the nation's businesses have computerized accounting systems, the number of bookkeeping and accounting clerks will change very little. Optical scanners, electronic mail, computers that recognize speech, and word processing will decrease the number of positions for data entry keyers and typists.

Marketing/Sales Occupations

In terms of the *number* of employees, more workers will become retail salespersons than will join any other occupation. Jobs in retail sales will increase by 730,000. However, many people are already employed in retailing, and the *rate of growth* is only slightly greater than average.

More than 300,000 workers will become cashiers, but escalating use of automated pay-point machines will greatly limit this job's growth. More and more, retailers will have electronic cashiers which take orders and charge the purchase to the customer's bank or credit card.

On the other hand, prospects for securities and financial services sales representatives and travel agents are bright. Rising personal incomes will increase the funds available for investment, and banks and other financial institutions will offer an expanding array of financial services. Vacation and business related travel will increase, building stronger demand for air travel. American business is expected to increase the average number of vacation weeks annually.

PROJECTED GROWTH TO 2000 FOR MARKETING/SALES OCCUPATIONS

Occupation	Number of Employees in 2000 (Thousands)	Change in Employees (1988-2000) (Thousands)	Percent Change (1988-2000)
Retail Salespersons	4,564	730	19%
Cashiers	2,614	304	13%
Securities/Financial Services Sales	309	109	55%
Marketing/Advertising/ PR Managers	511	105	26%
Travel Agents	219	77	54%
Real Estate Agents/ Brokers	445	64	17%
Retail/Wholesale Buyers	220	13	6%

Source: Bureau of Labor Statistics

Health Care Occupations

Jobs in Health Care will account for more than one-sixth of total job growth. The number of registered nurses will increase by 613,000, the second largest increase of any profession. More than 550,000 health technicians and almost 380,000 nursing aides will be added to the labor force.

An aging population, broad medical insurance coverage for many citizens, increased complexity of care, and emphasis on out-patient services will contribute to this growth. Patients will undergo more tests, see more specialists, and be subjected to more comprehensive treatments than ever before. However, there will be continued attempts by the business and government sectors to limit increases in the cost of health care.

PROJECTED GROWTH TO 2000 FOR HEALTH OCCUPATIONS

Occupation	Number of Employees in 2000 (Thousands)	Change in Employees (1988-2000) (Thousands)	Percent Change (1988-2000)
Registered Nurses	2,190	613	39%
Health Technicians	2,211	566	34%
Nursing Aides	1,562	378	32%
Home Health Aides	397	160	68%
Physicians	684	149	28%
Medical Secretaries	327	120	58%
Pharmacists	206	44	27%
Physical Therapists	107	39	57%
Psychologists	132	28	27%
Dentists	189	22	13%

Source: Bureau of Labor Statistics

Food Service Occupations

Higher incomes and more leisure time will allow people to dine out more often. As a result, food service occupations will expand greatly. Furthermore, many of these jobs experience substantial turnover, which will create numerous replacement openings.

PROJECTED GROWTH TO 2000 FOR FOOD SERVICE OCCUPATIONS

Occupation	Number of Employees in 2000 (Thousands)	Change in Employees (1988–2000) (Thousands)	Percent Change (1988–2000)
Chefs/Cooks/Bakers	3,341	586	21%
Waiters/Waitresses	2,337	551	31%
Food Counter Workers	1,866	240	15%
Food Preparation Workers	1,260	234	23%
Food Service/Lodging Managers	721	161	29%
Bartenders	506	92	22%

Source: Bureau of Labor Statistics

Construction Occupations

Construction activity will expand, although the increase will be slower than in the past. However, growth will vary significantly for different types of construction. A slowdown of population growth, as well as a slowdown in the formation of new households, will limit residential construction. But industrial building construction will increase as manufacturers develop new factory technologies and build new facilities to capitalize on these advances. The current oversupply of office and commercial buildings will be absorbed during the early 1990s, and then more of these facilities will be erected.

PROJECTED GROWTH TO 2000 FOR CONSTRUCTION OCCUPATIONS

Occupation	Number of Employees in 2000 (Thousands)	Change in Employees (1988–2000) (Thousands)	Percent Change (1988–2000)
Carpenters	1,257	175	16%
Electricians	638	96	18%
Construction Helpers	633	78	14%
Plumbers/Pipefitters	469	73	18%
Painters/Paperhangers	501	70	16%
Roofers	147	24	19%

Source: Bureau of Labor Statistics

179

Manufacturing Occupations

Manufacturing will lose more than 300,000 jobs by the year 2000. Improved production processes, robotics, better machine sensing capabilities, and technological innovations will precipitate declines in most professions. However, a few manufacturing jobs will grow modestly.

PROJECTED GROWTH TO 2000 FOR MANUFACTURING OCCUPATIONS

Occupation	Number of Employees in 2000 (Thousands)	Change in Employees (1988–2000) (Thousands)	Percent Change (1988–2000)
Metal Workers	1,030	61	6%
Industrial Production Managers	254	39	18%
Plastic Molding Machine Operators	176	32	22%
Woodworkers	249	22	10%
Welders/Cutters	309	–16	–5%
Machine Feeders	218	–31	–13%
Electronic Equipment Assemblers	91	–71	–44%
Machine Setters/ Operators	4,779	–170	–3%

Source: Bureau of Labor Statistics

Transportation Occupations

Most transportation vocations will have average growth in the next decade. More freight will be shipped, so more truck drivers will be needed. A greater number of automobiles will be on this nation's roads, but longer intervals between routine service operations will restrain growth in the jobs for automotive mechanics. Fewer workers will be needed for railroads as they become more technologically advanced.

PROJECTED GROWTH TO 2000 FOR TRANSPORTATION OCCUPATIONS

Occupation	Number of Employees in 2000 (Thousands)	Change in Employees (1988-2000) (Thousands)	Percent Change (1988-2000)
Truck Drivers	3,024	382	14%
Automotive Mechanics	898	126	16%
Bus Drivers	593	88	17%
Bus/Truck/Diesel Mechanics	312	43	16%
Rail Transportation Workers	90	−16	−15%

Source: Bureau of Labor Statistics

183

Agricultural Occupations

Although demand for food, fiber, and wood will increase as our population grows, more productive farming and consolidation of smaller farms will result in declining employment in many of these occupations. However, opportunities for gardeners and groundskeepers will grow as people desire more leisure time and as more recreational facilities are built.

PROJECTED GROWTH TO 2000 FOR AGRICULTURAL OCCUPATIONS

Occupation	Number of Employees in 2000 (Thousands)	Change in Employees (1988–2000) (Thousands)	Percent Change (1988–2000)
Gardeners/ Groundskeepers	943	182	24%
Agricultural/Food Scientists	30	5	21%
Foresters/Loggers	139	−6	−4%
Farm Workers	785	−153	−16%
Farmers	875	−266	−23%

Source: Bureau of Labor Statistics

The Fastest Growing Occupations will Require the Most Education and Training

In the year 2000, jobs will be available for many people who are not college graduates. For example, retail salespersons, cashiers, receptionists, secretaries, and waiters and waitresses will experience numerous job openings.

At the same time, receiving a college degree will not guarantee that one's profession will grow rapidly. The number of college faculty will expand very slowly because college enrollments will peak in the 1990s.

However, employment will generally increase faster in occupations requiring the most education and training. Health care vocations and computer related jobs will undergo rapid expansion. Most technical and professional occupations will grow more quickly than the average for all vocations.

Furthermore, college graduates, on average, earn more than workers without college degrees. In 1987, the median salary for all college graduates was $31,029; the median salary for all workers with a high school diploma was $18,902. Managers with college degrees earned $37,252, while those with high school educations earned $23,286.[1]

Even workers with jobs requiring few specialized skills will have to read and write, have fundamental math skills, follow instructions, and speak clearly. So while employment opportunities will be available in a variety of occupations, workers with the highest levels of education and training will have a competitive advantage over those with less education, and they will have more options in the job market. Access to higher paying jobs will be particularly restricted for workers with less than a high school education.

CHANGING MANAGEMENT STYLES

♦ By eliminating many middle management positions, a leading steel producer reduced its salaried workforce by 70%.

♦ The manager to worker ratio of a major office equipment manufacturer has gone from one to seven in the early 1980s, to one to twelve in 1990. By the year 2000, it will increase to one to eighteen.

♦ "Flatter" organizational structures will mean reduced opportunities for vertical promotions. In order to keep employees content, companies will have to redefine the meaning of "success" during the 1990s.

"Flatter" Organizational Structures

During the 1980s, many large companies discovered they could operate better by eliminating numerous supervisory levels which had been built up over time. These multiple organizational layers had been slowing down communications. Large companies were unable to make decisions quickly enough within an increasingly complex environment. Middle level managers who left these firms were not replaced.

In the 1990s, this trend toward "flatter" organizations will continue. As more companies participate in competitive global markets, they will realize that, in order to remain on top, they must operate as efficiently as possible. The method of streamlining operations that will produce the most immediate results will be to reduce layers of middle management. Some firms will do this through attrition and not replacing those managers who leave. Others will take more active and immediate steps to trim their middle management.

Technology has also contributed to reducing intermediate management positions. More than ever, personal computers and an electronic information workplace have allowed workers to access the knowledge and data that enables them to participate in decision making. Thus, the role of manager is changing from that of an autocrat to that of an organizer and mutual participant in the decision making process.

Changing Management Attitudes

"Flatter" organizational structures have precipitated a change in management attitudes. As middle level supervisory positions are eliminated, more responsibility has been given to the remaining workers. "Empowerment" and "Employee Involvement" became buzzwords of this evolution, and workers were viewed more as part of a team, rather than as people to take orders.

Another factor in the progression of management styles has been a change in employee attitudes toward their jobs. Instead of viewing a job as a drudgery that must be endured to earn a living, employees who have been given increased responsibilities are deriving more satisfaction from the work they accomplish. A Human

Resources Vice President commented:

Workers today are looking more at job satisfaction, rather than merely looking at receiving a paycheck.

Today's employees are more likely to question the duties they are assigned and the way in which tasks are to be carried out. Workers want to provide input into how the job might be best accomplished.

An executive from one of America's leading manufacturing firms said:

Businesses are moving away from an authoritarian style of management. This is a trend that started in the 1960s. Employees are starting to ask "why". Management styles are becoming more persuasive. The workforce is being treated with more dignity; they are being given more credit for their intelligence.

Participatory Management and the Empowerment of Workers

In the 1990s, companies will continue to shift away from authoritarian styles of management. Managers who traditionally gave orders for the workforce to follow will become leaders who organize workers' efforts to accomplish business goals.

Close interaction between managers and employees will characterize the workplace of the future. More authority will be given to workers farther down the organizational hierarchy. Lower level employees will become more involved in problem solving and day to day decision making. Accountability will fall on the shoulders of everyone in the company. Some distinctions between hierarchies of workers and management will blur as authority is delegated to more workers.

Furthermore, workers will have greater flexibility in the methods they use to accomplish their tasks. Management will specify objectives, and then give employees latitude in their approach to achieve those goals.

A major American industrial equipment manufacturer summarized this participatory management in the following way:

Workers in the future will be more involved in making decisions about issues that are closely related to their jobs. They will not make decisions about what companies the business will acquire, but they will be involved in those decisions that affect their day to day tasks. This is not an adoption of Japanese quality circles or management styles, but it is a reaction to competition with overseas businesses. This competition spotlighted how smug some American companies were about their positions and made them realize they must improve. American businesses require better working relationships with their employees to remain competitive in the face of foreign competition.

In a labor market characterized by shortages of educated and skilled workers, a climate that emphasizes manager-employee interaction will be a valuable recruiting tool. With greater participation will come a feeling of accomplishment and more job satisfaction.

Companies who have already implemented a participatory management style said that employee reaction to these changes has been positive. A large office equipment manufacturer commented:

When these changes are made properly, there is a tremendous increase in worker satisfaction because they have greater responsibilities. Workers have less supervision from middle managers, but they receive more feedback directly from customers or from the work process. However, to recognize and reward their empowerment, employees must share in the gains they create.

A More Active Upper Management

As the number of management layers are reduced and the workplace becomes more participatory, upper management will become more active. Rather than sending directives through subordinates, even top managers will find themselves interacting with lower level workers. Managers will spend more time leading group discussions and getting feedback from workers.

They will be asked to explain company goals and policies. As one corporate Vice President put it:

> *Lower level employees will see that upper management does not just sit in their offices and go to lunch. Upper management will take a more active management role.*

The successful manager will be one who can communicate with the workers. With more interaction among employees and clear explanation of company goals and procedures, communications will assume even greater importance within the organization.

Already, companies are recognizing that communications will be a key to successfully reducing layers of management. A Human Resources executive said:

> *When levels of supervision are reduced, the reaction of lower level workers will depend on how well the manager can relate to the workers. If middle management is eliminated, top management must get out of their offices and meet with the hourly workers. They must do a better job of communicating with workers. This is an area of real concern.*

Fewer Vertical Promotions

"Flatter" organizations will result in reduced opportunities for vertical promotions. As levels of management are trimmed, positions to which deserving workers would have been promoted are eliminated. Competition for higher positions that do open up will intensify. Advancement up the organizational hierarchy will be limited for all but the most exceptional employee.

Management of larger American companies will be faced with a great dilemma: How to satisfy the expectations of an enormous number of workers who will want to move up vertically within their organizations.

In the year 2000, almost 70 million workers will be between the ages of 35 and 54. Another 32 million will be 25 to 34 years old. As the U.S. workforce matures, workers will be looking to join or move up the ranks of management.

Since the opportunities for vertical promotions will be scarce, the competition for management positions will escalate. How will businesses keep their workers from becoming frustrated and angry when they remain at the same organizational level? How will employees who are unable to move up the hierarchy keep from viewing themselves as failures?

Redefining the Meaning of "Success"

Traditionally, "success" has been viewed as advancing up the management ladder. But with reduced vertical promotions and fewer workers moving up the organizational hierarchy, large businesses must redefine how their employees perceive success. Otherwise, workers stuck in the same position will not be as productive as they could be, and neither workers nor the company will operate at maximum efficiency.

The Vice President of a large semiconductor manufacturer summarized the situation this way:

Organizations must define "advancement." There must be a dual ladder where workers contribute as individuals and where they progress in the company through opportunities. The public must change its traditional view of success and we must value individual contributions more. Also, there must be more job rotation to offer workers a variety of tasks. Job rotation and different tasks have an enormous effect on job satisfaction.

Large companies will have to clearly explain to their employees the reason for a lack of opportunities for vertical advancement. They will have to make it clear that it is a question of demographics and economic survival. For the company to prosper, it must reduce the layers of management and hold down costs. At the same time, a maturing workforce means more workers will be wanting to move into higher positions. Lack of promotion must not be associated with "failure".

Rather than viewing success as vertical promotion, workers will have to be reinforced or rewarded in other ways. Employees will have to derive greater self-satisfaction from the job. Being given more power to make decisions and more accountability is one way to increase job satisfaction.

Workers can become leaders of project teams, propose ways to better carry out the company's operations, perform special assignments, or evaluate the ideas of others.

Job satisfaction will also come from mastering a variety of challenges. Workers will be assigned a broader array of tasks or more lateral assignments. Instead of being specialists, employees of the next decade will be generalists.

Companies will do more to publicly reward individual and team contributions of their employees. Trophies, acknowledgements in company newsletters, press releases in community newspapers, being honored at company banquets, and awards such as "employee of the month" will recognize those who made significant achievements.

Some companies may also reward their best employees with incentives such as one time bonuses, or increased vacation time in lieu of promotions.

If workers feel that an employer values their contributions, most will stay with that company, even when the prospect of vertical promotion is bleak. However, some people will be satisfied with nothing short of a promotion. More workers blocked from advancing up the management ladder of large companies will lead to more people joining smaller firms or becoming entrepreneurs. At the end of this decade, fewer people will be employed by large firms.

Influence of Overseas Management Styles

With an increasing number of foreign firms dominating world business, a greater proportion of the workforce will be employed by firms headquartered outside the United States. Some multinationals will operate with sharply different management styles than U.S. workers are used to, while others will allow their American operations to be managed autonomously and let local mangers decide their own management styles.

When foreign multinationals acquire U.S. operations, for the near term, they usually continue operating as before. This is to avoid losing valuable personnel who are concerned that operations will change too rapidly for their liking. But after some time, foreign management styles will often be imposed. It will be natural for multinationals to want to impose their own management style on U.S. operations so that their worldwide organizations will operate most efficiently.

FUTURE BENEFIT PACKAGES

♦ Employers will be doing more in the 1990s to attract and retain the most highly skilled workers. At the same time, they will trim benefits which do not give them a competitive advantage.

♦ **More companies will allow employees to choose from a "cafeteria style" selection of possible benefits.**

♦ **Vacation time, educational benefits, child care, elder care, legal assistance, vision care, and other benefits will increase.**

♦ **Current pension fund payments and retirees' benefits will be reduced during the 1990s.**

♦ **Medical care will be a benefit category under intense scrutiny in the 1990s.** Companies will increase deductibles, and firms' own medical clinics will provide the first line of health care in an attempt to trim escalating health care costs.

Salaries

The foremost benefit influencing an employee's decision to join a company, or to continue there, will remain salary levels.

Leading Human Resource managers felt that **salaries for workers in established jobs will generally increase at an annual rate 2 to 3 percent above inflation during the 1990s.**

However, higher salaries will be paid to employee groups who can fill coming key shortages in the workforce:

♦ Graduating college seniors, who will be in short supply throughout the 1990s.

♦ The upper 20% of high school graduates not intending to go to college, but who have the aptitude and desire to fill key technician positions.

♦ Experienced people of retirement age who can be enticed to remain on the job from one to five years longer to relieve the Skill Gap.

♦ Employees in technical or professional occupations experiencing a shortage of qualified workers.

In the 1990s, companies will be less likely to pay competitive wages for mediocrity. With technological tools in place, white collar workers will be able to out perform their counterparts of just a decade ago. Companies equipping their executives with the latest advances will expect ever increasing performance. As one leading Human Resources Manager stated:

Companies will be stressing pay for performance and sticking with it more in 1990s. There is more of a tendency for employers to stick by the incentive plans they set and not give low performers pay raises.

There will be a more disproportionate salary reward system, with top performers and workers in key labor shortage categories receiving much higher salaries.

The 1990s will see a greater use of bonus programs, spot awards, team awards, etc. to reward exceptional performance in a more timely manner.

Vacation Time

One benefit which will be increasing during the 1990s will be vacation time.

The annual two week vacation is still the standard vacation time allowed by the majority of U.S. companies. Additionally, most employers provide employees with further vacation time annually based on the total number of years they have worked with the company.

♦ Typically, employees with many years in service will receive 5 or 6 weeks off per year. But very often, all of this time is not taken. The responsibilities of a person's position often do not allow them to take all of the vacation time they may have earned each year. Therefore, many companies allow employees to accrue vacation time from one year to the next up to certain limits.

However, in many other countries, vacation time has already far exceeded typical United States levels.

♦ In Australia, 6 weeks off is considered a standard. In Europe a combination of vacation time, more holidays, and personal days very often makes 5 or 6 weeks a standard. Additional weeks for seniority can be added.

With many fringe benefits being taxed during the 1990s, employers are going to stress those benefits which will be less subject to taxation as a fringe benefit. **Extending the amount of vacation time given per year will become one of the major benefit evolutions of the 1990s.** It is a benefit which the government cannot easily tax, and one which fits in with the Wellness programs being fostered by many companies because of its potential for reducing stress.

By the year 2000, a second year American employee will find that 3 to 4 weeks annual vacation time per year will be a standard. However, for senior employees the time taken off is unlikely to exceed six weeks. At a management level, more time off will dramatically interfere with job performance and the employer's increasing expectation that problems be addressed more and more quickly in this high tech world.

One executive with a leading chemical company said recently:

> *If I take my full allotment of vacation time each year, I won't get my job done. And one of the times when I get back from a three week vacation, my job will have radically changed, or may be eliminated. I can't afford to be that out of touch with the office.*

Length of the Work Week

The majority of personnel managers contacted during the research phase of this book agreed that it is very unlikely that the nation will see a significant reduction in the standard 40 hour, 5 day work week.

Through the years, a number of employers have experimented with shifting work schedules to shorten the length of the Friday workday, or to create a 4 day, 40 hour work week. These employers largely feel that the net result of these schemes has been unsatisfactory.

Three primary reasons why a 40 hour, 5 day work week will remain a standard in the 1990s are:

- ♦ The trend has been to reduce the size of organizations, letting the remaining workers do more with the increased technology available. They will not be able to fulfill all their new responsibilities in less than a forty hour week.

- ♦ We are working in a global economy. Decisions are made and transmitted across the world to customers or suppliers within the hour. Most of the rest of the western world works at least a five day week. The Japanese, Taiwanese, and Koreans often work a six day week. U.S. companies will not be able to unilaterally go to a four day week. They would miss too much.

- ♦ Organizations are often driven by the results of meetings. It will be harder to organize the right people to come to these meetings with a four day week, or a staggered schedule. Each week key executives have a certain amount of time set aside for meetings and the remainder set aside for implementing the decisions made at these meetings. Human Resource Managers believe that in a four day week, key people will be too busy to do both.

Medical Care

One of the most valued benefits traditionally awarded employees has been medical benefits. However, in the past decade these expenses have risen so astronomically that many employers are actively considering ways to reduce the cost of this benefit.

As the Human Resources Manager of a leading Aerospace company reported:

> *In 1980 we paid 27 cents per $1 of salary for medical benefits per employee; in 1990 it will be in the vicinity of 35 cents per dollar of salary. We just cannot afford further increases in the health care benefit, and expect to stay competitive when bidding for international jobs.*

Employers in the 1990s will be seeking to trim their outlays for health care benefits. Many believe that they can accomplish this without harming the true value of this benefit category through better management. Here is how it will be done:

♦ Lower premiums can be obtained from insurance companies by increasing the annual deductible (the amount of medical payments the employees have to pay themselves before they can submit claims for reimbursement). An increase in the deductible from $200 to $500 can dramatically cut the monthly premium. When further increased to $1,000 per year, the savings are even more dramatic, leaving the employee with essentially catastrophic coverage at a relatively low premium. The insurance company does not have to act on numerous small claims, so they can pass on the savings to the employer.

♦ Employers will be required to pay some part of their health care through "coinsurance" provisions which require the employee to pay a portion of hospital or other costs.

One study found that the proportion of plans where the employer provided complete reimbursement of hospital room and board charges decreased dramatically during the 1980s. The same study indicated that employers were requiring pre-admission testing, second opinions on surgery, and asking employees to elect outpatient surgery where possible.[1]

211

♦ Many people in their twenties do not utilize their insurance to the extent of their older counterparts. A large deductible might suit them very well. The cafeteria style benefit plans, which will be discussed shortly, are allowing companies to recognize this for the first time. By providing young employees limited insurance to cover catastrophic medical or accidental situations, companies can offer employees alternative benefits of greater interest.

♦ Today, when many employees are sick they take off from work and spend half a day waiting around doctors' offices, etc. to be examined for five minutes and told they have the flu, or some other routine ailment. A prescription is then written and the employee spends another hour or so waiting to get it filled. Many firms are planning to bring back a version of the company clinic as both a first line of defense against illness, and as the focal point of Wellness Programs.

One medical benefit which will be increasing is that many companies will begin to offer vision care (eyeglasses, and exams) in addition to dental care, which is now routine. Almost everyone has some kind of vision care requirement after they reach age 40 or 45. This type of additional medical benefit is one which a majority of major companies are considering.

Another major trend will to be cut back on medical benefits provided to retirees.[2] One of the actions which started this is a complicated series of moves made by the government which would have made employers change their tax treatment of these benefits. Some major corporations have already cut back or are planning to in the near future.

Health Care Providers

Many employers of the 1990s will require that employees first visit the company clinic, before applying for outside medical benefits. Thus, they can limit outside medical expenses to more advanced diagnostic procedures. They can also use the clinic to routinely monitor employees' overall health, and thus help detect potential high blood pressure, diabetes, or other problems before they become catastrophic. Annual, or biannual employee physicals will often be conducted at the company clinic, where their costs can be controlled.

Employees coming into the workforce of the 1990s will be required to utilize the company clinic approach, or at least a company HMO.

Some workers have traditionally, preferred to select their own medical facilities. Companies installing more comprehensive medical clinics are going to have to convince their employees to use the facility. As one executive put it:

Upper management needs to be particular about the clinics they set up for the company. They need to pay more attention to how the clinics are staffed and how they are equipped. This is going to have to be done so well that all employees will feel comfortable going in there. If our executives can have a problem attended to in a first class manner and with efficiency, then the other workers are not going to object to using the facility.

The clinic staff is going to have to get across the point that they are operating only as a first line of defense, and if there is any doubt to the diagnosis, then patients will be allowed to go to the specialist of their choice.

Among smaller companies, Health Maintenance Organizations (HMOs) and Preferred Provider Organizations (PPOs) will experience an increase in popularity.[3] HMOs provide basic medical services for a fixed fee per employee per month. PPOs allow an employee to chose their own doctor, with a variable fee per service.

In the past, HMOs have had difficulty selling the service of a group of specific doctors because some workers have preferred to select their own medical facilities and staff. PPO programs offered by the same organizations can help supply an alternative.

Wellness Programs

Wellness programs will be another "benefit," or service which the company clinic will very likely be providing. Companies are going to become more and more involved in educating their employees about good health habits. This will become one of the routine functions of the company clinic. Each month the company clinic will develop an educational theme to be stressed in company training programs.

Typical Wellness Program themes will be:

- **Smoking**
- **Obesity**
- **Alcohol**
- **High Blood Pressure**
- **Cholesterol**
- **Annual Physical Exams**
- **Stress Avoidance**

With these programs, the company clinic can aid in preserving the health of company employees. When a firm is large enough to support a clinic, tremendous savings can be gained on health care premiums.

Additionally, there will be significant demand for HMOs to bring wellness programs to their client companies in the form of brief educational seminars and descriptive material. Those that can provide this kind of additional service will have a marketing advantage in the 1990s.

One outgrowth of wellness programs will be to continue to reduce the number of company facilities where smoking is allowed. Another benefit will be to provide increased awareness of environmental factors in the workplace which might damage a worker's health.

Child Care

Federal tax law now authorizes a percentage credit for expenditures on child care up to a maximum of $4,800 for the care of two or more qualifying dependents (only up to $2,400 for a single dependent). The government also allows qualifying companies to reimburse their employees up to $5,000 annually (only $2,500 if married filing a separate return) for all dependent care expenses without being taxed.[4] However a tax credit cannot be claimed for any portion of employer paid care.

As one leading Human Resources manager stated:

> *The federal government has put an indirect tax on virtually all working families with several children. In many cases both spouses have to go to work to attain an improved lifestyle. We have lots of working families who, with overtime and both spouses working, earn more than $50,000 annually. They are allowed only 20% of the amount actually spent as a credit. Or if they are taking our benefit package they can only take $5,000*

before they have the surplus taxed as a fringe benefit at the highest salary rate they will be earning that year.

This benefit should be based on the number of children actually receiving child care, it should be exclusive of income level formulas.

There has been considerable debate about whether companies will have more on premises child care. A minority of companies have established on site child care facilities into their company facilities with mixed results. Sometimes workers abuse the privilege and come down to visit their children too many times a day. Despite some abuses, company child care facilities will very likely increase in the early 1990s. This will be done in order to accommodate the large number of women expected to be returning to the workforce during the 1990s.

Providing child care benefits is presently difficult for many smaller employers. One competitive idea to boost occupancy rates in the many empty or partially filled office buildings in the nation, would be for building management to provide the child care facilities in their building. If these offices are filled with smaller companies, their employees could utilize the facility.

Children under school age could come to the same building as their parents, and mother or dad would be close by in case of an emergency, or if they felt the need to visit their children during the day. A building's management can easily test relative demand before getting involved, by sending out a questionnaire to their tenants.

Elder Care and the Sandwich Family

Several Human Resources managers estimated that their employees currently seek child care benefits over elder care benefits by a ratio of 20 to 1. However, as the population becomes older, elder care is going to become more important to employees.

In order to keep many of their best employees on the job, companies will have to offer benefits for elder care. A significant number of workers in their fifties and sixties have parents who have become their dependents and need special treatment. This older group will be opting for elder care benefits, and will rarely need child care.

According to Money Magazine,[5] there are an estimated 680 thousand families in the U.S. which are **"Sandwich Families,"** or families responsible for caring for both children and parents. In many cases, the grandparents can provide the equivalent of child care in the home, but too often they are in too frail of health to provide child care.

Families with this burden will prefer to receive both child care and elder care benefits.

Pension Funds

Pensions funds and capital accumulation programs were benefits which received major attention in the 1970s and 1980s. In the 1990s this emphasis will change. As one Human Resources Vice President stated:

> *The executive retiring in the 1980s or early 1990s has sometimes become so affluent that their net worth with pension funds and other accumulations very often exceeds a half million dollars. You simply can't appeal*

to these people to stay on the job. If we currently wanted to ask them to stay on, we would have to cough up a great deal to make it worthwhile. We are not going to continue making large pension fund contributions into the 1990s because during that decade, we are going to need some of the retirement age people to work a bit longer. If they are as comparatively wealthy as their predecessors, then we are going to have great difficulty retaining them.

Another reason for pension fund accumulations to decline is that during the late 1980s, the Federal Government limited allowable employer contributions to many pension fund programs, to no more than 15% of an employee's annual salary. This has stopped many companies who had a windfall year from paying their employees a large one time contribution. In the past, one or two extremely good donations in an executive's career, which accumulated tax free compounded interest until retirement, produced a comfortable nest egg.

Legal Assistance

Legal assistance for common needs such as wills, trusts, and property transfers is an additional benefit that can be easily provided by an employer's law department. Employees in their 50's and 60's will find this benefit of increasing importance.

Taxable Versus Tax Free Benefits

Many of the traditional perks of company executives were eliminated after the tax reform act of 1986 or other legislation. For example, after this date, companies were allowed to deduct only 80% of an executive's meals taken on the road. Most chose to simply let this expense deduction go, but companies might conceivably take the whole deduction and have their employees report the 20% of total travel meal reimbursements as additional income for tax purposes.

Other perks have also come under scrutiny, and might be subject to taxation, unless they are handled very carefully, and recipients in many cases will have to prove a primary business use. These include:

- **Travel rewards.**
- **Company cars.**
- **Club memberships.**
- **Tuition reimbursement.**
- **Child care reimbursement above certain limits.**

Now many benefit deductions are in peril by virtue of section 89 of the 1986 tax reform legislation.[6] The intention of this law was to eliminate the disparity between the value of benefits given to workers of different wage levels. Unless there is further legislation, the criteria of the present and immediate future is that all employees will have to share in a benefit to the same extent or it may not be deductible.

During the 1990s employees at all levels will find that an increasing amount of their benefits will be subject to taxation. This will usually appear on W-2 forms as Fringe Benefits, which will be reported to the IRS by employers.

Employees will come to find that they payout comparatively little money on a taxable fringe benefit. For a higher income employee who receives $1,000 in fringe classified benefits, he or she (in 1989) will have only paid out $330 in federal taxes, plus applicable state taxes. This still makes a very good deal, provided the employee puts a high value on the benefits received.

It is conceivable that employees may not favor the benefits that they receive enough to even want to pay the taxes due on them. Perks, like travel, may be resented if they are received as part of an award that the employee may not particularly want. They might want to travel to a different location, or just have the time off.

♦ In the area of both formal benefit programs and fringe benefits, employers of the 1990s are going to have to be a lot more open to giving their employees choices, to ensure that they are happy with their benefits. A great many benefits will be offered as choices in a "cafeteria style" program.

The Golden Handshake

Another benefit being given to esteemed employees is a last career move before they retire. For example, an employee may be awarded a transfer to Hawaii, or Florida if they postpone retirement for two years.

Another form of the golden handshake is to provide an increased pension fund contribution for extending the retirement date a couple of years. Employees delay receiving their benefits and receive a couple more years' contribution while they are working. This increases their pension base while they are earning the highest salary of their career. Additionally, with just the right retirement date, they can sometimes collect an entire year's additional contribution for only a partial year's work.

Many other forms of the golden handshake will become standard practice during the 1990s as employers seek to persuade valued older employees to extend their careers.

"Cafeteria Style" Benefits

By the mid 1990s, **"Cafeteria Style,"** or **"Flexible Benefit Packages,"** will comprise the heart of most employee benefit programs. They will represent a way in which employers can still customize for individual need, yet treat all employees equally. This is a feature of benefit programs mandated by the Federal tax reform act of 1986. This equality of benefits doctrine will very likely be with us for the 1990s even if there is another sweeping tax reform.

♦ In terms of attracting or keeping valued employees, the menu allowed in a flexible benefits package will evolve into the most important benefit, other than base salary, that an employer will possess in attracting or retaining good workers.

By early 1990, approximately one third of all major U.S. corporations were offering their employees a choice of benefit packages.[7]

There are several driving forces behind the popularity of cafeteria style benefit programs:

♦ A desire to give employees benefits that will be more useful at each stage of their career.

♦ A need to prevent duplication of health care or other benefits in multiple income families.

♦ An effort to comply with Federal legislation which requires that all employees receive equal benefits in order for them to be tax deductible.

Cafeteria style benefit programs allow the employee to receive benefits as long as they sum to the same value. In many cases some benefits can be included in the package which might previously been subject to taxation. There is usually a cap of $5,000 per employee per year on the total value of the package of cafeteria style benefits which can be offered to each employee to choose from. The particulars of these programs must pass government scrutiny and approval.[8]

Provisions of the cafeteria style programs usually provide that an employee must commit to their selection at the beginning of the year and stick with it for the year to come. He or she cannot suddenly decide that they want dental benefits in place of eye care. Employees making the wrong choices at the beginning of the year will have to pay for any expenses themselves.

Two types of cafeteria plans are being served up: **Structured and Open**.

♦ In **Structured Cafeteria Plans,** the company may offer a set number of alternatives. For example, plan A will have catastrophic health care, plus some tuition reimbursement, and child care, all in certain defined amounts. Plan B might have more comprehensive medical coverage to include eye, and dental care, plus pharmaceutical costs. Plan C might include elder care, plus medical care for dependents, and minimal health coverage for the employee.

♦ In **Open Cafeteria plans**, the company defines all the benefits and puts a dollar amount on each of them. Then the employees are allowed to choose how much of each they want. The components chosen cannot add up to more than a set maximum per month which might be $300 or $400 depending on the employers budget.

One of the difficulties of cafeteria style plans is that they are going to require considerable expertise to get the details of each program approved by the government. Unless the government makes an effort to simplify the rules, it will be very difficult for a smaller company to set up and get approved.

Another barrier to small company participation is that insurance companies frequently require a minimum of 5 to 20 employees to set up group health insurance plans. The provisions of almost any cafeteria style plan will necessitate that several different levels of medical plans be provided from which each employee can select. Smaller companies may lack the sheer number of employees to provide the numbers needed to make a successful cafeteria style benefits program work.

Insurance companies and others will need to come up with a more flexible insurance product which provides the variable coverage needed by small companies. A possible future product for insurance companies or others might be to set up preapproved, standardized flexible benefits programs for their client companies to adopt.

Benefits by Age Appeal

Because of the importance which cafeteria style programs will be attaining, it will become necessary for employers to know which kinds of benefits will have the most appeal to various age groups. Also, since more fringe benefits are likely to be taxed in the 1990s, employers need to pay close attention to the likes and dislikes of particular groups of employees so that they do not try to provide unpopular benefits which might be subject to taxation.

For example, the younger sectors of the workforce will be most interested in high starting salaries, tuition assistance, and child care. Older employees will be more interested in medical benefits and pension funds; the most senior will favor more medical care, elder care, life insurance, and estate planning.

Shown on the next few pages is a summary of benefits likely to have the most appeal to various age groups. The listing is based on the collective wisdom of a number of the nation's leading personnel managers. However, there are always exceptions. For example, a couple in their forties may have a young child, or a person in their twenties may have a dependent parent with failing health, etc.

One of the great challenges of today's personnel managers will be to listen to their employees' needs and concerns, and to create a benefits program which will fulfill as many of these as possible. Modifications may have to be made to the program each year.

The Appeal of Employee Benefits to Various Age Groups

20's

♦ The major appeal to the first time job holder will be **starting salary**. This reflects a concern, particularly among recent college graduates to see their worth recognized in terms of dollars. Because of the coming skill gap, employers will have to pay higher initial salaries than ever before to attract the most talented from among this group.

♦ The youngest generation of workers will also be very interested in **knowing what they will be doing within the organization five and ten years from now.** In other words will the new employee be recognized, and advance within the organization - is there a plan? An employer needs to anticipate this concern, and to answer this question satisfactorily in order to attract the best of the new workforce.

♦ **Tuition or other forms of educational assistance** is very important to certain high achievers in this age group. The fact that they can have a large proportion of their tuition reimbursed while they receive additional education has a very high value. For college aspirants this may mean getting financial help to complete a bachelors or associates degree. Certain workers may value good technical skills training more than a good starting salary, knowing that the salary will increase once they have the foundation of a skill. Most young people do not plan on staying with one employer for a lifetime, they are looking to acquire skills so that they can advance when the opportunity presents itself.

♦ Another concern of a young employee is **portability of benefits.** Are the benefits they receive going to be transferable if they make a change of employers? Young employees frequently have a paranoia about becoming trapped in a job. Pension funds, life insurance, and other long range benefits are of minimal importance and are considered more remote.

♦ **Medical benefits** beyond catastrophic coverage for accidents, etc. are not important to this group at large. Individuals with a particular early health problem will naturally place more emphasis on medical benefits. Employers can test new applicants in the company clinic and, if no major health problems show up, may decide to allow them to take a $1,000 deductible medical insurance, so that they can concentrate on benefits which may hold more importance for this age group.

♦ An **opportunity to travel, and/or have a company car** are of very high value.

_____*30's*_____

- ♦ **For parents, pre and post natal care and child care benefits** are extremely important. **Pension funds** begin to take on more importance in their late thirties.

- ♦ Providing **flexibility of benefits to avoid duplication** of benefits with a working spouse has high appeal.

- ♦ **Matching savings programs** for capital accumulation are also of great importance, so that a first home can be purchased.

- ♦ **Dental care** is usually desired with increased medical benefits.

- ♦ **Portability of benefits.** Concern for what happens to their benefits if they change jobs.

- ♦ **Company fringe benefits and perks.** Travel, company car, club memberships, executive washroom key, etc. and fancy job titles are especially important to the single person in this age group as a way of establishing status among peers.

_40's_

♦ **Medical benefits,** particularly those relating to the future, or extending to the entire family.

♦ **Parental care benefits.** Nursing home, elder care benefits. Finding places for parents to live in retirement years.

♦ Help with **educational expenses of children.**

♦ **Savings plans, capital accumulation plans.**

♦ **Life insurance.**

♦ Often it is necessary for employers to **provide a new career path for high achievers** in this age bracket who are beginning to fear that they will not be able to realize their goals in a current job.

50's

♦ **Pension plan benefits** are of major importance.

♦ **Capital accumulation, savings plans.**

♦ **Elder care - nursing home protection.**

♦ **Medical care** has become more important.

♦ **Part time employment possibilities** for those whose working spouse is providing sufficient income.

♦ **Life insurance.**

_____60's and Older_____

♦ **The amount of coverage they will have at retirement age** is of paramount importance.

♦ **The possibility for a reduced number of hours of work** is extremely attractive to many of them.

♦ **Estate planning help.**

♦ **Life insurance.**

CONCLUSION

In the 1990s, America's Changing Workforce will find:

♦ **An Enormous Skill Gap**

♦ **A Maturing Workforce**

♦ **A Greater Proportion of Women and Minorities**

♦ **Rapid Technological Change**

♦ **A Shorter Life for New Products**

♦ **A Declining Share of the World's GNP**

♦ **An Expectation that Each Worker will Accomplish More**

♦ **Sweeping Changes in Management Styles**

♦ **Reduced Opportunities for Vertical Promotion**

♦ **Changing Salaries, Benefits and Work Schedules**

These influences and changes are interdependent. Each of them will have an enormous effect upon on the way we live and work in the 1990s. The only driving force which we possess the power to correct over time is the enormous Educational Shortfall which we have acquired as a nation. If we can improve upon that one short-coming, many of the situations described in this book will fall more in our favor.

For individuals, correcting the Educational Shortfall will mean keeping up with the day to day challenges and changes which Technology will bring into our professional lives. It will mean paying closer attention to the educational achievement and goals of our children. It will also mean lending a hand to help others outside the immediate family so that they can fulfill their own potential.

NUVENTURES
CONSULTANTS, INC.

NUVENTURES began operations in downtown Chicago in May, 1975. Since that beginning, the company has received most of its recognition from its industrial market research capabilities. A great many of these assignments evaluated the economic consequences of new products, ideas, or strategies, before sizable client investments were committed.

Very often, NUVENTURES assignments have involved an analysis of new technologies. The company has already completed assignments relating to many of the technologies discussed in Chapter VI of this book.

Early in the company's history, NUVENTURES began to accept international assignments. Since a first Canadian assignment in 1977, staff members have traveled to over thirty countries to conduct projects. By telephone survey, market research has been conducted in many additional countries of the free world. A total of nine languages have been utilized to conduct these international assignments.

NUVENTURES' established client base includes multinationals headquartered all over the world. Over 50 of these clients have sales exceeding one billion dollars annually. Each year well over 90% of NUVENTURES assignments come from an already established client base.

In 1983, NUVENTURES moved its operations to La Jolla, a pleasant seaside community within the city of San Diego, California. This location enabled us to better serve our international business.

_____CHAPTER ENDNOTES_

_____PREFACE_

OUR EVOLVING WORKFORCE _____CHAPTER I_

EDUCATIONAL CHALLENGES _____CHAPTER II_

[1] National Commission on Excellence in Education, *A Nation at Risk* (Washington, D.C.: U.S. Government Printing Office, 1983),

[2] Hudson Institute, *Workforce 2000,* (Washington, D.C.: U.S. Government Printing Office, 1987), p. 98.

[3] Reich, Robert B. 1988. *Education and the Next Economy.* Washington, D.C.: National Education Association, p. 19.

[4] Based on data resulting from studies by Educational Testing Service. Used by permission.

[5] *A World of Differences: An International Assessment of Mathematics and Science,* © 1989, Educational Testing Service, p. 14. Used by permission.

[6] Reich, Robert B. 1988. *Education and the Next Economy.* Washington, D.C.: National Education Association, p. 25.

CHAPTER II - continued

[7] U.S. Department of Education, National Center for Education Statistics, *Projections of Education Statistics,* (Washington, D.C.: U.S. Government Printing Office, 1989), pp. 67-68.

[8] Hudson Institute, *Workforce 2000,* (Washington, D.C.: U.S. Government Printing Office, 1987), p. 98.

[9] U S WEST Education Foundation, 720 Olive Way (Suite 1725), Seattle, WA 98101.

[10] Robert B. Reich, 1988. *Education and the Next Economy.* Washington, D.C.: National Education Association, p. 19.

CHAPTER III

AN AGING WORKFORCE

[1] Hudson Institute, *Workforce 2000,* (Washington, D.C.: U.S. Government Printing Office, 1987), p.76.

[2] Howard N. Fullerton, Jr., "New Labor Force Projections, Spanning 1988 to 2000," *Monthly Labor Review,* November, 1989, p. 10.

[3] Ibid, p. 8.

[4] Andrea Rock, "The Truth About Post-Job Jobs," *Money Magazine (Time Inc.),* Money Guide, Fall, 1989, p. 76.

[5] Ibid.

[6] Hudson Institute, *Opportunity 2000,* (Washington, D.C.: U.S. Government Printing Office, 1988), p. 155.

CHAPTER IV

WOMEN IN THE WORKFORCE

[1] Howard N. Fullerton, Jr., "New Labor Force Projections, Apanning 1988 to 2000," *Monthly Labor Review*, Nov. 1989, p. 5.

[2] Ibid., p. 4.

[3] Sharon Nelton, "The Age of the Woman Entrepreneur," *Nation's Business*, May 1989, pp.23-24.

[4] Sharon Nelton, "Six Ways to Be 'Family-Friendly'," *Nation's Business*, March 1989, p. 13.

[5] International Labour Office (Geneva, Switzerland), *Conditions of Work Digest*, Vol. 7, Feb. 1988, p. 290.

[6] Ibid.

THE GROWING IMPORTANCE OF MINORITIES

[1] Susan Tifft, "The Search For Minorities," *Time*, August 21, 1989.

[2] George Silvestri and John Lukasiewicz, "Projections of Occupational Employment, 1988-2000," *Monthly Labor Review*, Nov. 1989, pp. 42, 63.

[3] Los Angeles Educational Partnership, "Overview of Program Initiatives, 1984-1989," p. 3.

[4] Partners in Public Education, "Pipeline to the 90's," *PipeLines*, December 1989.

CHAPTER V - continued

[5] Los Angeles Educational Partnership, "Overview of Program Initiatives, 1984-1989," p. 3.

CHAPTER VI
TOMORROW'S TECHNOLOGICAL DEVELOPMENTS

[1] "Lasers Used to Weld Tissue," *High Technology Business*, June 1989, p. 31.

[2] Carolyn Hlavaty, "Trends," *Personal Computing*, Oct. 1989, p. 189.

[3] Computer Daily, "GE Teaches Computers to Read--And Understand," *High Technology Business*, July-August 1989, p. 31.

[4] Paul Bonner and Marty Jerome, "CD-ROM Power: Knowledge in Hand," *PC/Computing*, Vol. 3, No. 2, Feb. 1990, p. 67.

[5] Advanced Military Computing, "DOD Funds Optical Computer for Early 1990s," *High Technology Business*, Sept.-Oct. 1989, p. 35.

[6] MFOC Newsletter, "Fiber Optics Used to Control Aircraft," *High Technology Business*, July-August 1989, p. 34.

[7] "Sun Sufficient Solar Cell," *High Technology Business*, Sept.-Oct. 1989, p. 9.

[8] Ron Bel Bruno, "Conversational Computing," *Personal Computing*, August 1989, p. 32.

[9] Alexandra M. Biesada, "Tooth Tech: The New Dentistry," *High Technology Business*, April 1989, pp.28-29.

CHAPTER VI - continued

[10] Jeffrey Zgymont, "3-D Printers," *PC/Computing*, Feb. 1990, pp. 123-124.

[11] Gordon Graff, "Profiting From Electronic Photography," *High Technology Business*, May 1989, p. 23.

[12] Michael Antonoff, "Computing is the Medium for the Message," *Personal Computing*, Oct. 1989, p. 168.

CHAPTER VII
THE FUTURE WORKPLACE

CHAPTER VIII
THE CHANGING SHAPE OF U.S. BUSINESS

[1] *Handbook of Economic Statistics,* U.S. Central Intelligence Agency, 1989.

[2] *National Accounts,* United Nations Statistics.

[3] "Top 50 Banks in the World," *The 1990 Information Please Almanac,* (Houghton Mifflin Company Boston), p. 57. Based on data from *American Banker,* July 24, 1989.

[4] "Outlook Economy," *Changing Times,* January 1989, p. 36. Based on data from Data Resources, Inc.

[5] "Union Membership of Employed Wage and Salary Workers, 1985," *Monthly Labor Review,* Sept. 1985, p. 44.

CHAPTER VIII - continued

6 "Current Population Survey," by Bureau of Census, for U.S. Department of Labor, Bureau of Labor Statistics, (Washington, DC 20212: USDL 89-45).

7 Ronald A. Taylor, "Tomorrow - Why Organized Labor is Unlikely to Make a Comeback," *U.S. News & World Report*, Sept. 11, 1989.

8 "Labor - Unions Must Woo Young and Women," *USA Today*, August 1989, p. 10.

9 Ronald A. Taylor, "Tomorrow - Why Organized Labor is Unlikely to Make a Comeback," *U.S. News & World Report*, Sept. 11, 1989.

10 "Labor - Union Must Woo Young and Women," *USA Today*, August 1989, p. 10.

11 "Current Population Survey," by Bureau of Census, for U.S. Department of Labor, Bureau of Labor Statistics, (Washington, DC 20212: USDL-45).

12 "Labor - Unions Must Woo Young and Women," *USA Today*, August 1989, p. 10.

13 Charles C. Heckscher, "A New Work Force Needs New Representation," *Work in America*, Work in America Institute, Sept. 1989, Vol. 4, No. 9, p. 2.

_____*CHAPTER IX*
OCCUPATIONAL SHIFTS

[1] George Silvestri and John Lukasiewicz, "Projections of Occupational Employment, 1988-2000," *Monthly Labor Review*, November 1989, p. 63.

_____*CHAPTER X*
CHANGING MANAGEMENT STYLES

_____*CHAPTER XI*
FUTURE BENEFIT PACKAGES

[1] "Employees Bear Larger Share of Health Costs," *Work in America*, Work In America Institute, Sept. 1989, Vol. 24, No. 9, p. 6.

[2] Janet Bodnar, "Make the Most of Your Fringe Benefits," *Changing Times*, Sept. 1989, p. 93.

[3] Cheryl Besemer, "Managed Health Care Programs Can Ease Skyrocketing Costs," *San Diego Executive*, May 1989, p. 18.

[4] Form 2441 and Instructions, Department of the Treasury, Internal Revenue Service (Washington, D.C.: U.S. Government Printing Office, 1989).

[5] Eric Schurenberg, "The Crunch of Caring for Both Parents and Kids," *Money*, March 1989, p. 93.

[6] Janet Bodnar, "Make the Most of Your Fringe Benefits," *Changing Times*, Sept. 1989, p. 96.

CHAPTER XI - continued

[7] Lani Luciano, "Company Plans: The Tax Break You Shouldn't Ignore," *Money,* Nov. 1989, p. 127.

[8] P. Garth Gartrell, "Strategy: Painless Employee Raises," *San Diego Executive,* May 1989, p. 32.

CHAPTER XII

CONCLUSION

NUVENTURES

PUBLISHING

In January 1990, NUVENTURES® Consultants, Inc. formally started its publishing division. The first book to be published was "America's Changing Workforce - About You, Your Job, and Your Changing Work Environment."

NUVENTURES' second book will be a historical action adventure and spy story set in the British Isles during the American Revolution. It is called, "Henry Lunt and the Ranger." It is a fictionalized account of an actual incident involving one of the voyages of John Paul Jones. $5.95 ISBN 0-9625632-2-6

In the future, NUVENTURES® Consultants, Inc. may author additional business and other titles. We have already conducted extensive market research involving the potential popularity of a number of topics.

NUVENTURES may be willing to consider publishing the work of outside authors. If an author or their agent wishes to have NUVENTURES consider publishing their book, **the following procedures must be strictly followed.** First, obtain a copyright number for the completed manuscript through the Library of Congress, Washington, DC 20559. Then send a typed one or two page synopsis of the manuscript together with a copy of both sides of the "Certification of Copyright Registration" complete with its registration number to:

Topic Reviewer
NUVENTURES Publishing
P.O. Box 2489
La Jolla, California 92038-2489.

If the Topic Reviewer has a potential interest in your manuscript, you will be contacted. At that time you would be asked to send your complete manuscript for review. **Please do not send us unsolicited manuscripts or suggestions for books which have not been completed.** We regretfully will have to immediately discard any submissions which are not provided in strict accordance with the above procedures. SAN 200-3805

HENRY LUNT & THE RANGER

TOM McNAMARA

HENRY LUNT & THE RANGER
April, 1778

An infant American Navy is struggling to gain recognition in the courts of Europe. Ambassador Benjamin Franklin has ordered Captain John Paul Jones to capture a British fighting vessel of "at least similar or greater size" than his American corvette Ranger.

Jones rescues long time sailing comrade Henry Lunt from a Welsh prison. Immediately, he lands Lunt ashore in Ireland to find out why the British Sloop of War Drake, despite his taunting, remains steadfastly at anchor deep within Belfast Harbor

But the French know that the Drake has been chosen by the British Admiralty to test a new secret naval weapon, one that could alter the balance of power in Europe for decades to come. The French want the Drake to remain where she is, until they alone can steal her secrets. They have little regard for the interests of a fledgling American nation.

Over the dinner table of the Royal Navy, the interests of a young American naval officer and a French master spy collide. The spine tingling naval action which follows in the Irish Sea will make you an immediate fan of the Henry Lunt series.

BOOK ORDER INSTRUCTIONS

If you are unable to find our books at your local store, you may purchase books direct from NUVENTURES® Publishing by mail, by FAX, or by Telephone using your VISA or Master Card number. Complete the form on the reverse side of this notice and

MAIL a check, or complete the credit card information and remember to sign the order form.

> To: Personal Book Orders
>   NUVENTURES Publishing
>   P.O. Box 2489
>   LaJolla, CA 92038-2489

FAX   the completed credit card information and include your personal telephone number for verification:

> Book Order FAX: 619-459-0569

TELEPHONE 1-800-338-9768 and have your credit card information ready when you call. (see reverse side)

SPECIAL DISCOUNTS FOR LARGE VOLUME ORDERS FROM SCHOOLS & CORPORATIONS

Quantity discounts are available with bulk purchases for educational, business, or sales promotional use.   Write to: Discount Sales Department, NUVENTURES Publishing, P.O. Box 2489, LaJolla, CA 92038-2489.

MAIL or FAX
BOOK ORDER FORM
(see instructions on reverse side)

Qty	Title	Per Unit	Totals
____	**America's Changing Workforce** About You, Your Job, and Your Changing Work Environment	$12.95	$ _____
____	**Henry Lunt and the Ranger**	$5.95	$ _____
	Book Subtotal		$ _____
ADD: California or other Applicable State Sales Tax			$ _____
ADD: Shipping/Handling Charges per order			$ _2.00_
	TOTAL		$ _____

Account Number   Expiration Date (Month, Year)

VISA: _____   _____

Master
Card: _____   _____

Ship to: _____
Please Print

_____

_____

_____
City - State - Zip

Signature: _____

Telephone: (___)_____

BOOK ORDER INSTRUCTIONS

If you are unable to find our books at your local store, you may purchase books direct from NUVENTURES® Publishing by mail, by FAX, or by Telephone using your VISA or Master Card number. Complete the form on the reverse side of this notice and

MAIL a check, or complete the credit card information and remember to sign the order form.

To: Personal Book Orders
      NUVENTURES Publishing
      P.O. Box 2489
      LaJolla, CA 92038-2489

FAX the completed credit card information and include your personal telephone number for verification:

Book Order FAX: 619-459-0569

TELEPHONE 1-800-338-9768 and have your credit card information ready when you call. (see reverse side)

SPECIAL DISCOUNTS FOR LARGE VOLUME ORDERS FROM SCHOOLS & CORPORATIONS

Quantity discounts are available with bulk purchases for educational, business, or sales promotional use. Write to: Discount Sales Department, NUVENTURES Publishing, P.O. Box 2489, LaJolla, CA 92038-2489.

MAIL or FAX
BOOK ORDER FORM
(see instructions on reverse side)

Qty	Title	Per Unit	Totals
___	**America's Changing Workforce** About You, Your Job, and Your Changing Work Environment	$12.95	$ ___
___	**Henry Lunt and the Ranger**	$5.95	$ ___
	Book Subtotal		$ ___

ADD:
California or other Applicable State Sales Tax $ ___

ADD: Shipping/Handling Charges per order $ 2.00

TOTAL $ ___

Account Number   Expiration Date (Month, Year)

VISA: _____

Master
Card: _____

Ship to: _____
Please Print

_____

_____

_____

City   -   State   -   Zip

Signature: _____

Telephone: (___) _____